MISSION: THE SMALL CHURCH REACHES OUT

ANTHONY PAPPAS
SCOTT PLANTING

Judson Press ® Valley Forg

Mission: The Small Church Reaches Out

© 1993

Judson Press, Valley Forge, PA 19482-0851

Bible quotations in this volume are from the NEW REVISED STANDARD VERSION of the Bible, copyrighted 1989 by the Division of Christian Education of the National Council of the Churches of Christ in the United States of America, and are used by permission. All rights reserved.

Excerpt on pages 25–27 from A SIMPLE HONORABLE MAN by Conrad Richter
Copyright © 1962 by Conrad Richter. Reprinted by permission of Alfred A. Knopf, Inc.

Printed in the U.S.A.

Library of Congress Cataloging-in-Publication Data
Pappas, Anthony.
   Mission : the small church reaches out / Anthony Pappas, Scott Planting.
      p.   cm. — (Small church in action)
   Includes bibliographical references
   ISBN 0-8170-1174-9
   1. Small churches. 2. Mission of the church. I. Planting, Scott. 1950–   . II. Title. III. Series.
   BV637.8.P367   1993
   250—dc20   93-1337

To Marsha Planting
and

To my dad, Charles G. Pappas,
who first taught me about faithfulness
and mission,
and
to Eleanor Long,
who is in heaven making sure God
gets the jots and tittles right!

Foreword

Small churches are in a class by themselves. To overlook their uniqueness is to misunderstand them.

Unfortunately, small churches are commonly misunderstood. For example, they have long been viewed as proving grounds for new pastors. According to that assumption beginning pastors should make their mistakes in small churches; fewer people are involved and, therefore, the mistakes will be less costly. Also, those who demonstrate their ability in ministry with small churches will likely be effective pastors of larger churches.

Such viewpoints are hardly warranted. Only the most crass perspective could hold that those who are members of small churches deserve consistently lower-quality, less-experienced pastoral care than those who are members of large churches. Small churches are not smaller versions of large churches. They are qualitatively, as well as quantitatively, different. The insights pastors gain in ministry with small congregations do not transfer directly to larger congregations. In my own experience those who minister well and are happy in a small church rarely are as happy or effective when they move to a large church. Church members who are nurtured and who are effective lay leaders in small churches rarely find similar nurture or are as able to serve when small churches become larger.

Small churches deserve to be dealt with in their own right. Denominational programs in education, outreach, stewardship, etc., designed for large churches rarely suit the needs of small congregations. To draw the potential out of small congregations, those who lead them and who provide resources for them need to appreciate their potential as small churches.

This series of books is designed specifically for those who lead and support small churches. Each author is someone who cares about and understands the unique possibilities of small congregations.

Tony Pappas and Scott Planting are uniquely qualified to write this book about the mission potential of small churches. Tony's ministry with the First Baptist Church on Block Island demonstrates that even isolated small churches have immense capacity to serve their communities. Scott's twenty years of experience guiding the outreach efforts of twelve small churches that compose Mission at the Eastward provide a sound basis for the rich insights he shares. Both authors demonstrate grounded vision in this book. Their faith in God and vision for small churches come through on every page. But they are equally well grounded in the day-to-day realities of small-church life. Their book offers practical vision for small churches in mission.

Douglas Alan Walrath
Strong, Maine

Contents

Acknowledgments

As I anticipated, it was fun and growthful working with Scott Planting and Doug Walrath on this book.

My gratitude to Suzanne Wagner, who in typing this manuscript had not only me to deal with but also every other piece of malfunctioning equipment in our church office.

My appreciation to the people of the Harbor Church, Block Island, Rhode Island, for being such great and humble missioners for Christ.

My hat off to countless faithful small-church folk who are making God's kingdom a little bit more real in every corner of the globe.

—*Tony Pappas*

My appreciation to Doug Walrath for his help with this project.

My thanks to Kara Ohlund for typing the manuscript, and to Russell Kaniuka for editing the text.

My appreciation to the Mission at the Eastward and the parish I have served for two decades: Fairbanks Union Church, Farmington, Maine; New Portland and North New Portland Community Churches, New Portland, Maine.

—*Scott Planting*

Introduction

Dialogue and Definitions

Doug Walrath: The first two questions the reader is going to want to have answered in a book like this are, What is a small church? and, What do we mean by mission?

Tony Pappas: I know a small church when I feel it.

Scott Planting: And I know mission when I see it.

Walrath: Let's hear some specifics from your own experiences with small-church life and mission.

Pappas: Actually, Scott, you know mission before you see it. You see it when it isn't there and then you make it happen. Why, the housing ministry of your small parish in rural Maine is a miracle in itself—and the electronics assembly plant you and your fellow dreamers brought into being. And what about the dialogue your church people started between management and union during the paper strike?

Planting: And Tony, you know a small church when you feel it—yours on Block Island and the scores of others you've visited—but you also know how to THINK small church, how to comprehend it, understand it, wrestle with it, and move it towards greater faithfulness.

Pappas: Yet in every instance of need around you, Scott, God seems to have presented an opportunity for response—an empty factory, a burned-out family desperate for housing—and you focused the energy of the people around you to respond actively, whether it was helping one neighbor or changing a region's economy.

Planting: Right. God takes the lead and is present in all dimensions of reality.

Walrath: So we can define mission as *participation with God* in the transformation of human life—individual, corporate, and institutional.

Pappas: Now, Scott, your congregation has come to expect this kind of involvement. It's part of who you are; it's your way of doing things.

Planting: Right, and that's your point about the nature of the small church. In American culture a small church is often incorrectly seen as a diminutive, voluntary organization when, in fact, it is a face-to-face society, a culture-bearing organism—a tribe, I think you call it. It's a living entity in which persons and relationships are the foremost reality. People have a sense of "we-ness" and have developed traditions and language that reinforce their common identity. The essence of the small church is its sense of social wholeness—community.

Pappas: As Peter put it so well: You are a face-to-face society, a Kingdom culture, "a chosen race, a royal priesthood, a holy nation, God's own people [tribe]" (1 Peter 2:9, NRSV).

Walrath: But some people think the term "small-church mission" is an oxymoron, a contradiction, an impossibility. So let's get started helping people understand that small churches can indeed carry out effective mission as God provides opportunities.

Chapter 1

Different and Do-able

Six Keys to Understanding Small-Church Mission

As authors, it is our firm belief that:

- The small church *does* do mission. We intend to open your eyes to a fresh perception of mission that will reveal the small church as central to God's purposes.
- The small church *can* do mission. We will demonstrate that mission is as central to the nature of the small church as survival *when mission is understood biblically, not culturally.*
- The small church can be encouraged to greater faithfulness in its mission efforts. We will share understandings, approaches, and strategies that work in the small church because they are consistent with the unique nature of the small church.

There are over 330,000 congregations in our nation, about two-thirds of which are categorized as small churches. Within these small churches are a variety of attitudes and approaches to mission involvement. However, it is apparent that all too often people within and outside of small churches believe that small churches can't *do* mission. More importantly, if we small-church people believe them, it shows we have *chosen* to view ourselves not from God's perspective, but from society's.

We all know plenty of churches that are so internally focused, so full of lament and discouragement, so closed to what God is doing right outside their walls that they fall into the trap of believing they are incapable of doing mission. They see the limits of their resources, not the possibilities. And yet we also know many small churches that lead their area in mission giving, that provide soup kitchens and shelters for the homeless, that support foreign missionaries or run day-care centers or hospices.

Let me prick a small hole in the balloon of logic of the small-church naysayer. Let's pick at random 200,000 human beings. In that group there will be a murderer or two, a few dozen thieves, a few thousand who cheat on their income taxes, a few thousand who cheat on their spouses, hundreds who do drugs, many thousand who overdo alcohol, a number of spouse beaters and child abusers, thousands of neurotics, hundreds of psychotics, and so on and so on. One could get pretty down on humanity, and with good reason.

But also in our group will be some doctors making house calls or delivering babies at midnight, some teachers who care enough to give extra help and encouragement to even their slowest students; hundreds of parents who spend time with their children after a hard day of work and who stay up all night with a sick child; half a dozen men putting Bibles in hotel rooms in the belief that the Word of God can speak to every human need; dozens of people visiting shut-in neighbors to give a moment of light to an otherwise dreary day; a handful of men and women working against inconceivable odds to provide decent housing, preserve crucial environmental locations, or pursue justice in employment or race relations; and a few dynamic souls "trapped" in immobile bodies offering constant prayer for other human beings and God's creation.

Now, if one chooses to say on the basis of this sampling of humanity that people are self-focused and self-indulgent, the evidence is there. Yet within this same group one could point to incredible examples of self-sacrifice, self-giving, idealism, constancy, love, maturity, and service. Further, even the murderer in our group would have been touched by some of these qualities. One could get pretty up on humanity, and with good reason.

So which is the right choice? Which does God choose? Well, there's no doubt about it. God chooses to be up on humanity. And that's the perspective we need to choose in approaching the small church and its mission activity. We must see the small church as a form chosen by God to effect divine mission in the world. This choice will not be easy or simple because the dominant culture in our society seemingly values opposite choices, and bureaucratic organizations such as our denominational structures at many points reflect a worldview more in line with the dominant culture than the small church's. In addition, small churches often view themselves as powerless victims in this arena.

Exploding the Myth

Myths are not so much folk or fairy tales as they are stories or scripts that give shape to the reality of the people holding them. Myths are true if you believe them. That is, by believing them, you make them true. But myths can be false if the truth they purport conflicts with the way God would have things.

There is a myth operating that gives shape to the small church's mission, a myth held both by those outside the small church who embody a different view of reality than people in small churches do and by small-church people themselves. But this myth is false, and it devalues the mission of the small church. It needs to be replaced by an understanding of the centrality of the small church to God's intent.

The myth, stated simply, is: The small church can't do mission. It has certain variations: (1) The small church *won't* do mission. (Said disparagingly, with the unspoken message, "You could if you wished to, but you don't. You are bad Christians, selfish and unteachable.") (2) The small church *doesn't do* mission. (Said plaintively with lament and regret, and with the unspoken parental message, "Oh, we had such high hopes for you, but you just won't grow up. Shame on you.")

Of course, there are many who don't buy this script, and many others who buy the script but are working all the harder to encourage mission activity in their small church. However, the myth must be taken seriously because of its pervasive presence in American church life, and because it has implications for the ways small churches see themselves.

For example, there is a danger that small-church people may feel left out or overlooked by their denomination, as if they are not really there. (A pastor of a small church complained to me that one of his denominational executives had coffee weekly with the pastor of one of the large churches but failed even to return his calls.) This feeling may lead people to conclude: "We can get along fine without the denomination. What good are they to us anyhow? We'd be better off using the money here."

Carl Dudley shares an amusing, if sad, experience.

> In my work on a denominational committee, I was introduced to what's known as supporting churches, churches that received subsidies to enable them to carry out particular programs. In an effort to qualify for funding support, these churches had to provide mission statements describing their proposed programs. The purpose of the committee meetings was for denominational staff to discuss new programs and emphases in the denomination. They would discuss a new youth kit or a new women's organizing manual or a new evangelism program, and so on and so forth. The leaders from the churches would then return in a couple of months with their mission statement. I was very impressed with their commitment and their discipline, but their presentations began to be similar, like a song with different verses but the same refrain: "O Lord, give us three more years. Then we can make it on our own and become a real church."
>
> It was really kind of sad because after they left, the long-time members of the committee explained to me that the

programs would never make it. I wondered why they wouldn't make it, and they said that small churches were afraid of change and afraid of outsiders and afraid of all sorts of things. That struck me as very odd, because I had grown up in a small church and I knew the direction in which fear flowed. I knew elders in those churches who could freeze a teenager in midflight. For them to be afraid of anything made no sense. I said there must be some mistake, and I decided that denominations had organized an opportunity so that the denomination could misunderstand the small church and vice versa.[1]

Differing Perspectives

The mutual misunderstanding and the need to learn a new language (recurrent small-church experiences) corroborate the fact that the denomination and the small church are two different social entities. Though both are valid in their own right, they are poor interpreters of each other. It will be helpful to attempt to articulate some of the differences in perspective resulting from their differences as social structures.

Church bodies beyond the local level are bureaucratically structured. This is not a pejorative statement but a descriptive one. That is, they are social structures organized by bureaus, departments, and hierarchies. In contrast, small local churches are organized according to their personal and highly traditional nature. This means that each lives in a distinct social world. We can start to describe these two worlds by contrasting their perspectives of four realities: mind-set, time, actions, and purpose.[2]

Mind-set

An organization's basic mind-set influences its overall perspective. In a bureaucracy the basic mind-set is vertical; talk of "climbing the ladder" and "career track" is frequent and fitting. In the world of the small church, the mind-set is horizontal; the world is something to be experienced and lived in without considering an upward dimension.

Time

Denominations as a whole also differ from the small church in their perception of time, for denominations tend to emphasize what is going to happen *tomorrow*. From this perspective, planning and preparation are crucial. But in the small church, what is really important, what gives meaning to life, is what happened *yesterday*. The accumulated wisdom of preceding generations is valued.

Actions

Where ought the behavior of the group to come from—habit or rational goal setting? The fundamental sin from a bureaucracy's point of view is the tendency of humans to lapse into patterned behavior (what we did this time last year) rather than to think everything out. But in the small church's point of view, the basic sin is the notion that a person can solve the mystery of life by thinking. According to the small-church perspective, the accumulated wisdom of preceding generations is the basis for determining behavior, with the understanding that modest adjustments can be made if necessary.

Purpose

Why are we here? What are we about? Are we here to change the world, to make a difference? Or are we here to experience and enhance the rhythms and relationships of life? Denominations may claim Psalm 90:17 as their motto: "Let the favor of the Lord our God be upon us, / and prosper for us the work of our hands." In contrast, small churches may claim Ecclesiastes 3:2-3 as their motto: "A time to be born, and a time to die; / a time to plant, and a time to pluck up what is planted; / a time to kill, and a time to heal; / a time to break down, and a time to build up."

These four perspectives are all facets of the differences between the small church as a social system and the national ecclesiastical structure as a social system. Each has its God-given place, and neither is evil or wrong per se. But when the differences are not acknowledged and appreciated, when one insists on broadcasting and receiving on its wavelength only, when the apples are taken to be oranges gone bad, then the myth arises: The small church can't (won't, doesn't) do mission.

Denominational personnel and small-church people must make every effort to develop two-way communication that will result in a truer understanding of the small church—its culture, capabilities, needs, and mission. Recognition and validation of the mission activity of the small church are essential for exploding the myths that "the small church won't do mission because it is not a significant entity in the life of the larger denomination," and "the small church can't do mission because it just doesn't have the resources or ability."

The tendency to think of the small church as a stepping stone to "success" in a larger church must be challenged and overcome. Likewise, the assumption (conscious or unconscious) that "bigger is better" or that a small church's only goal should be to become a larger church must be changed to a positive perception: The small church is valuable in and of itself, and its unique identity offers a perspective that needs to be clearly heard on the denominational level. The world of the small church is not a ladder to be climbed and conquered. Its world is flatter. Sure, it has its share of peaks and valleys, but it is not something to be climbed or even traversed. It is something to be lived in.

Sizism is the term David Ray uses in *Small Churches Are the Right Size* to describe the societal predisposition that bigger is better. To be small in America today is automatically to be on the defensive. The conclusion flows from the thesis: if bigger is better, then smaller is worse. Biblical people know this is not true, but faithful voices have been cowed into silence by those who are yelling the American thesis loudly with society's encouragement.[3]

And it doesn't end there. Not only is bigger better, but *increasing* is obligatory. It is not enough to be big; one must also

continuously be getting bigger. Bigger is better, but getting
bigger is best. Never can you rest on your laurels, for someone might be gaining on you, and only being the best is good
enough. This, of course, is a formula for failure. Even winners are losers under this scheme. The small church must re-
ject this myth. If we in the small church can do this, not only
will we be saved, but we will also be a force for salvation for
our lost society.

In filling out an annual report form for my denomination, I
felt that an implicit message—unintentional as it must be—
was that *doing* is what was important to them. I came to that
conclusion after checking the "no" box twenty-one out of
twenty-two times when asked to indicate which activities my
church engaged in. But I'm not so sure I agree that we exist to
do; I think it's vice versa. We do to exist. We do what we need
to do in order to keep and enhance our life together. Our doing is the service of our being. Doing is important, but being
is crucial. Isn't that why the church has always insisted on the
preexistence of the Christ? Jesus did not come to exist in the
doing of his mission, but from the very nature of his existence
flowed the Incarnation. So, too, in Christ's body, Christ's
church:

> From our identity comes our activity.
> From our integrity comes our service.
> From our being comes our doing.
> From our *koinonia* comes our concern.
> From our internal life comes our external mission.

Our being cannot be captured in the listing of our activities,
just as a personality cannot be captured in a photograph or a
daily "to do" list.

Someone once said that organizations are what they measure. Unfortunately for Christ's mission in the small church,
the denominational organization seems to be geared up to
measure observable doings, while small-church people tend
to register intangibles such as caring, faithfulness, and de-
pendability. We in the small church have listened to the voice

of society saying that what is real is what is countable, measurable; quantity is, in the final analysis, all that is real. But the small church values intangible, subjective qualities such as loving relations and doing the kind of mission with the right hand that the left hand can't see.

For many denominations, mission is perceived as programs. A program is a coordinated, scheduled activity moving toward a specifiable objective and requiring the organization of resources with quantifiable indices of achievement. A program is run. The one who runs it knows who is going to do what by when, how, and why, and how it will be known that what was to be done was actually done! Of course, many church-run programs are looser than this, but they are all capable of being formulated this way.

Programs *are* one form of mission. But so are giving a cup of cold water in Jesus' name, a spontaneous visit to a hurting neighbor, and a voice crying in the wilderness. These kinds of mission are not as easily registered and may be overlooked by those who document numbers of activities.

Recently my wife proposed that we go fix our elderly neighbor's back steps. Now we could (and I hope we will) do this. It will just be an act of Christian love, caring, and neighborliness. Or we could organize a home fix-it program in our church. (We could call it "Fix-Up Neighbor's Endangered Entrances," or FUNEE.) Then we could say that about four percent (my wife and I) of our congregation were involved in our home repair program. If we take the kids along next year, that will double the percentage. We could document that each repair project took an average of six person-hours, up substantially from last year (six hours to be exact). We could do all this accounting and submit a report. Or we could just go fix the stairs, in which case the person reading reports would never know. But I have a hunch God might.

For those with eyes to see, it is clear that the small church can do and does do mission. Small churches need to believe in themselves and know that God is truly present in them. They need to stop buying into the values and perspectives of a society that tells them that only bigger is better. Above all, they need to claim their unique opportunity for mission and go about it.

Mission—Small-Church Style

What is the type of mission congruent with the God-given nature of the small church? There are at least six touchstones of small-church mission that we can point to.

1. *Mission in the small church is personal.* It is caring from person to person. Sometimes we'll run programs or have program-like elements to our mission, but at its core mission in the small church is a personal thing. It is Christian people responding to needs that they feel in their hearts. It might not hurt to have the state unemployment figures in the bulletin on Sunday, but it will help more to mention that Bill just lost his job and ask what we can do about it. People caring about people. Christ's people caring about God's people. The small church caring about its neighbors. That's the guts of small-church mission.

2. *Mission in the small church is the connection of where we've been to where we are.* When considering its mission the small church should start by understanding its nature as Christ's body. Who are we? What is our story? Where have we come from? What gifts has Christ given us? What has faithfulness meant in the past? What do we have to offer our neighbors? What has made us feel the most satisfaction in service before? The call of God to minister in the present will originate in a spiritual understanding of the past.

So the small church can minister out of what it is—its nature, its character, its specific personality. From this self-knowledge comes a sense of what it has to give or what its neighbors need. An awareness that a small church has given much in the past and still has much to give today can be a basis for continuing to meet needs as they become apparent.

3. *The key to furthering mission in the small church is usually to be found in its present pattern of behavior.* Small churches are not as good at initiating new activities as larger churches, who

may have a younger, more upwardly mobile and professional membership. Small churches are comfortable in their habits, and one way to enhance mission in the small church is to honor long-held habits. People in small churches know themselves in their dependable actions. When mission actions become patterned, they will serve their neighbors for decades, even generations.

A group of older men in a church across the Sound from mine gathers one day a week to finish off the Christian education wing of their church. They serve Christ, help the Sunday school, and enjoy one another's fellowship. Now when the neighbor's home was damaged by lightning, how hard do you think it was to move their carpentry activities next door for a few weeks?

The women in our church are active in quilting and needlework. It's fun for them and provides a means of raising funds for the church. When I heard that the women's group from a Hopi Indian church we are in touch with was looking for quilt squares, I passed the information along to the women in my church. "Right up our alley," they said. In a matter of days, boxes of quilt squares were on their way to Arizona. Patterned behaviors are the ally—not the enemy—of small-church mission.

4. *Small churches are motivated to fill the gaps in their world.* When a rip occurs in the fabric of small-church life, energy is almost always released to repair the damage. While we can't always figure out how to right the wrongs in the Third World, we are motivated to keep our own world aright. When a loss occurs, love is poured out in tangible acts of support. An illness brings a seemingly unending line of home visits and casseroles. If someone drops out of the congregation, an effort is made to keep in touch.

Some people organize their lives by the compartmentalization principle, but not people in small churches. Some small-church people may have a limited world perspective, but it usually is an integrated perspective. Their world coheres or ought to cohere. To motivate "compartmentalized" persons, one attempts to persuade them that their mission slice is underdeveloped. To motivate small-church persons toward mission, one points out the presence of a rip in the fabric of their life together.

5. *By its very nature, small-church mission is organic, integral, and responsive.* It does not tend to be complicated, sophisticated, or totally dependent on organization. "If we had organized, we would have failed," said one of the Christians of small, rural LeChambon, France, which sheltered over five thousand Jews during World War II.[4] People in small churches are close to the point of need, so small-church mission efforts can be local and spontaneous.

I have friends who are active in a large metropolitan church whose congregation comes from thirty-one counties in three different states! This congregation is not uncaring, impersonal, and distant. It will provide a cup of cold water to its neighbors by opening a soup kitchen and shuttling people in from the suburbs to staff it. In contrast, the small church, organically rooted in its city neighborhood, village, small town, or country setting, responds to its neighbors' needs differently. The small church is likely to register the need sooner because it is the need of people with whom members rub shoulders day in and day out. It is likely to respond spontaneously by bringing over a casserole or a bag of groceries that very night or by sharing information about job openings for the next morning.

This kind of reaching out to help a neighbor is the caring of those who find themselves in the same boat. For small-church people there is no going home *from* the neighbor; there is only going home *to* the neighbor. The small church is close to the points of human need. It is close temporally, so its response can be "up close and personal." It is close socially, so its response can be "in culture." It is close existentially, so its response can cause not the distancing of charity but the bonding of familial love.

6. *Mission in the small church is a marginal, fragile enterprise.*

The small church lives at the margin. We are, for the most part, financially marginal. Concentrating on just paying the bills and keeping the doors open is sometimes looked on as "survival mentality," but it can actually be a place of great spiritual value. The margin is the place of miracles. Since the small church is not known for its planning or organizing ability, and since it cannot marshal great numbers of people or abundant resources, it is utterly dependent on God for accomplishing its divine mission. " 'Not by might, nor by power, but by my spirit, says the LORD of hosts' " (Zechariah 4:6).

The story of the feeding of the five thousand is to me a parable of small-church mission. The needs of humanity are represented in the crowd hungry for lunch. We may be tempted to say, "But what is that among so many?" However, the Lord says to us, "Bring whatever you have to me." The small church, like the young boy, must decide whether to consume the resources itself or offer them to the Lord. The resources of the small church often seem too trivial even to bother the Lord with, but when the small church responds in faith and offers all of its resources, meager though they may seem, God does miraculous multiplication. The results are out of all proportion to the resources!

Small-church mission efforts are fragile, too. They run on a shoestring budget at best. They come so close to collapsing that one person can make or break them, and often that is seen as a negative—the problem with small-church mission. ("Well, the pastor had another good idea for mission, but Deacon Jones squashed it again.") But it can also be seen as a tremendous positive. Since every small-church mission effort rides on the contribution of every single person, anyone—even you or I—can be used by God to effect mission through our small church. We don't have to wait for a committee report or a budget allocation. We just do it! Mission in the small church is marginal and fragile, and that is exactly what makes it an exciting and thrilling endeavor.

From Here

More than likely you have read to this point because you want to understand mission in and through the small church better and because you want to do something about it. Perhaps you are looking for a mission agenda and mission strategies. In the next four chapters we will examine the arenas of small-church mission activity. Each chapter will conclude with implementation strategies for small-church leaders.

Chapter 2

Small-Church Mission: Presence

Mission Begins As Prayer

The emerging focus of mission in the church today centers on the local congregation. Traditionally, we thought of *mission* as missionaries bringing the gospel of Jesus Christ to remote peoples who had never heard the Good News. The strategy and structure of modern mainline denominations were organized to get resources to distant mission fields. Though local churches supported this mission enterprise with overwhelming generosity, helping to establish churches, seminaries, hospitals, and schools all across the world, their role was largely passive, providing resources to church agencies that did mission.

Church commentators now describe a shift in mission focus. Today, churches are coming to see the mission field not as far away, but as local. Congregations are organizing food closets to feed hungry people in their community, and ministering to the spiritual needs of troubled people.[1]

The shift in mission focus from something "out there" to which we contribute money, to local, hands-on ministry requires that we rethink the role of the church. Now, the local congregation is on the front line of mission. Laypersons and clergy are no longer bystanders, but missioners actively participating in congregation-based outreach.

What is the local mission field? For nearly a generation congregations have been engaged in community mission projects that respond to the needs of the emerging "underclass." Congregations working together or independently have organized food closets, soup kitchens, homeless shelters, and substance abuse rehabilitation centers. In recent years, as a worsening economy threatens the middle class as well, a new mission field is emerging. Churches in middle-class neighborhoods have begun ministering to people within their own congregations who are overwhelmed with the demands of modern life. Workers are declared "surplus" by major companies and find themselves out of work after years of devoted service. The promise of technology to make more time for leisure has proven empty. The reality is that of one- and two-wage-earner households struggling to keep up an average standard of living for their families. People in and out of the church find themselves overstressed, isolated, and spiritually empty.

Responding to local poverty—both spiritual and material—is the new mission field of the church. Small churches that create intimate and caring communities are, in the words of Emily Chandler, "God's answer to today's spiritual hunger for connection."[2] We believe small churches that can identify and creatively respond to people's needs for community are on the cutting edge of the church's mission. Rather than understanding size as a negative, we believe small churches are at the forefront of the evolving understanding of mission: small units of devoted believers caring for one another and the needs of people around them. Indeed, small churches may have an advantage in identifying grassroots needs and responding to them quickly.

Small churches can equip themselves for the emerging mission of helping their neighbors. Ministries of caring and support—the strength of small churches—need to be intentionally offered to people in crisis. Many small churches have been so preoccupied with survival and the pressure to grow numerically that they have forgotten the strengths and gifts that can be used for mission. We believe that at this moment in history small churches are God's answer to people search-

ing for meaning in their lives. Our goal in this book is to help
your church discover its particular local mission.

Not every congregation will organize a food closet or advocate for the needs of homeless people, but every church, no
matter what its size, does have a mission. One very small
church we know mails out a simple, handmade card to the
people in the community for whom prayers were offered at
Sunday worship. The cards remind sick people and their families that they are not forgotten.

In preparing to do mission, the first task for the small
church is to describe its congregational life. To describe well
the life of the congregation is to uncover the unique narrative
of the church. That does not simply mean listing programs
and activities (though that is included), but exploring the congregation's identity, context, and process.

> *Program* is the sum total of the things a congregation
> does, including what is on its calendar;
> *Process* is the way the congregation does what it does:
> how its leadership works, how its people and groups make
> choices and relate to one another;
> *Context* is the congregation's setting in the community
> and in its denomination, the external forces that constrain
> or influence what the congregation and its members are
> and do; and
> *Identity* is that rich mix of memory and meaning that
> grounds the congregation, defining who it really is in its
> heart.[3]

The second task for the congregation as it seeks to discover
and define its local mission is to understand the community.
What are the needs of people in the surrounding block,
neighborhood, town, or countryside? Community needs may
be very clear—day care for working families—or more subtle—
loneliness and isolation. No one else can define local mission
for your congregation. Mission opportunities flow out of the
meeting of the unique story of your church with identified local needs. (For a description of this process, see chapter 5.)

We believe the local mission of your church takes place on
four levels:

1. The first level of mission is *Presence*. By presence we mean the simple and complex ways in which a congregation embodies and communicates the gospel to its community.

2. The second level of mission is *People*. This includes the ministry of people to people, as well as the caring that makes us human and that Christianizes our social environment.

3. The third level of mission is *Pattern*, the conscious effort of the church to live out a more healthy and righteous lifestyle.

4. The fourth level of mission is *Program*. Program includes the specific ways we organize resources to meet needs. Mission promotions are in this category, as are soup kitchens, day care centers, and advocacy of community issues.

These four levels of mission are not stepping stones, one building upon another. Each level of mission is important and valid unto itself. Our point is that small churches have undervalued their contribution to mission because they do not see what they already do as mission. Too often, we have believed that unless we are sending significant sums of money to denominational programs we are not engaged in mission. This is not to dismiss or undervalue worldwide mission endeavors, but rather to affirm that it is also important for each congregation to identify its own local mission. Small churches are not bystanders in mission, but active participants. Our experience suggests that congregations active in local mission endeavors are also active supporters in denominational programs. But the primary small-church mission field is at home, in their own neighborhoods and among their own people.

We now turn to a discussion of each of the four levels of small-church mission in some depth, beginning with mission as presence.

Level 1: Mission as Presence

A tall steepled church nestled in a deep Vermont valley, a gothic stone church crowded in a block of inner-city row houses, a handsome, brick church prominently located on Main Street in a town that has become a bedroom community for a city. What do they have in common? Each building was constructed for a single purpose, to worship God. Many activities might take place within the church buildings, an AA group, a health clinic, a youth volleyball league. But these buildings fundamentally differ from community centers, social clubs, or fraternal organizations. Whether simple or ornate, whether packed with exuberant worshipers or only a few faithful witnesses on Sunday mornings, each church witnesses to God, offering a message of hope, love, and reconciliation. It is a message not spoken through the architecture of any other building.

We define mission as *presence* as the message of hope the church communicates to its community. The mere existence of a church in the open countryside or in a blighted inner-city neighborhood can be a presence that communicates hope to farmers struggling to survive or families seeking to escape violence. Mission as presence is all the ways a congregation demonstrates the gospel in its corporate life.

Mission as presence has several facets that we want to explore now in this chapter: *symbolic presence, spiritual presence,* and *public presence.*

Mission as Symbolic Presence

Perhaps the most powerful symbolic presence in the mission of the small church is the church building itself. The building is a symbolic presence because "it participates in the reality beyond itself to which it points."

It has been said that the church was deliberately placed in the center of virtually every New England village and deliberately constructed with its spire pointing heavenward so that it would stand as a continual reminder of the God/human connection. I was shocked into silence one day while chatting on the street corner with a townsperson who has never ever worshiped in our church. She said, "You know I don't go to church. But still it is very important to me to know that it is there." Just being there kind of anchors things.[4]

Just the presence of that New England church "anchors things." We do not pay enough attention to the message that our church buildings give to the community. What impression does a church give to the person driving by it for the first time?

At one village church several of the men meet every Saturday to eat breakfast and then spend the morning mowing the lawn, caring for the grounds, and tending to repairs on the building. The man who organized the first Saturday work day forty years ago did so because he wanted to enhance the "church's face to the community." The "face to the community" presented by a church building can say much about how we feel about what goes on inside. Appearance reflects the congregation's sense of esteem, and tells whether it is a place where strangers are welcome.

Many churches have bulletin boards displaying the worship hour, the title of the Sunday sermon, the name of the pastor, and a telephone number for more information. But I also drive past churches whose bulletin boards are obviously neglected. Stick-on letters have fallen, information is not current. Consider using your church bulletin board as an opportunity for mission. Use it to describe your congregation, to announce meetings or special events, or to comment on a community concern.

A story about how powerful a bulletin board can be for a church's mission is described in Taylor Branch's history of the civil rights movement, *Parting the Waters: America in the King Years, 1954-63*. Martin Luther King, Jr., began his ministry in the Dexter Avenue Baptist Church of Montgomery, Alabama. His predecessor, who did much to prepare the congregation for the ministry of King, was the brilliant and provocative Vernon Johns.

One of Vernon Johns' first acts in Montgomery was to replace the tiny bulletin board atop the steps at the church entrance with a much larger one on the sidewalk facing

Dexter Avenue. In 1949, all Montgomery read there that Vernon Johns would preach the following Sunday on the topic "Segregation After Death." No doubt many whites cherished a private hope that the races would be separated in the afterlife, but the public notice invited suspicion.[5]

Sermon titles such as "It's Safe to Murder Negroes in Montgomery" prominently displayed on the sidewalk bulletin board directed attention to the deep, underlying racial tensions in the city which would explode to the surface when Rosa Parks refused to give up her seat on the bus and the young pastor of the Dexter Street church protested her arrest by organizing the boycott which changed the face of America. It is clear that *symbols have power.*

I shared the story of Vernon Johns' bulletin board messages with a minister whose mill town church had a prominent street-side bulletin board. The next week he replaced a faded poster with one proclaiming in bold letters "Faith Happens," to counter a popular slang bumper sticker. People took notice.

Consider using your church bulletin board also to announce what groups meet in the building: Alcoholics Anonymous, a day-care center, community health clinics. Such announcements communicate symbolic messages: "This church is open to the needs of people in the community," and "Everyone is welcome here."

Many churches have bells and carillons, as well as bulletin boards. In our town, a church on Main Street has a carillon that plays a hymn on the hour. In the midst of crowded work days, the carillon music reminds people of the message of the church, and our common calling to be a community.

The appearance of the church building, bulletin boards and signs, parking lots, bells and carillons all help contribute to a church's symbolic presence. What statement does your church's symbolic presence make? How would the people who see your symbolic presence describe the congregation that meets in your church?

Remember, symbols have power. Do not overlook the importance of symbolic presence in your church's mission.

Mission as Spiritual Presence

In the Gospel of John, Jesus said, "I have come that they may have life, and have it abundantly" (John 10:10). We define spiritual presence as all the ways a congregation—corporately and through individuals—demonstrates the abundance of life that Jesus promises.

Consider how the congregation in LeChambon, France exemplified spiritual presence. Growing out of their understanding of the gospel and their experience as a persecuted minority, this congregation's identity centered on being a *welcoming community*. That inner sense of spiritual presence became mission when the congregation welcomed large numbers of Jewish refugees into their fellowship during World War II. The congregation did not retreat in fear of the Nazi occupation, but lived the gospel by offering hospitality to threatened strangers.

Spiritual presence, then, is that inner vitality which radiates outward as a congregation lives the Good News. Spiritual presence becomes mission as this inner quality takes on concrete form in the life of the congregation or community. Mission as spiritual presence can be embodied in many ways in the life of the congregation. The following stories are different portraits of mission as spiritual presence.

Prayer as Spiritual Presence

The pastor of a small village church recalls a pastoral visit:

I called upon a man living in our town who was dying of cancer. On the sideboard in the kitchen I noticed a bouquet of fresh wildflowers, and a bowl of fruit. The man smiled and offered me an apple. He told me where the gifts came from. "Some women from the church came to visit me last night. They brought the flowers and fruit. One of them offered to wash the dishes. At first I thought they were going to try and "save me." I don't have much to do with their church. But they talked with me about cancer and dying. Mostly if people come they talk about the weather, or anything but the fact that I am sick. But these people really wanted to know how I was doing and if I needed anything. They didn't stay long. Before they left they said a prayer with me and they held my hand. No one had ever prayed like that with me before. Will you thank them and ask them to come again?

The women of the church visited their dying neighbor out of their conviction that Christ makes a difference in how we live and die. They brought to the visit with their neighbor a word of hope born out of their own deep inner spiritual conviction. Their simple act of compassion said, "this is the kind of people we are." They risked going to visit a neighbor whom they did not know even though they could have been turned away. But the genuineness of their conviction, what we are calling spiritual presence, communicated hope to the neighbor and was received as an unexpected blessing. People of faith visiting a sick neighbor is also the church in mission.

Caring as Spiritual Presence

Sam Samuelson walked into the worship service late. He found a seat in a rear pew and sat through the service. Right before the benediction he slipped out of the sanctuary. A few weeks later Sam returned, again arriving late and leaving before the benediction. The next time Sam entered church the matriarch of the congregation was ready for him. During the first hymn, Thelma moved out of her pew and sat next to Sam. "Who are you?" she asked. "Why do you leave? Let me introduce you to the minister and some of the people. Please stay." Thelma wouldn't let Sam slip out that Sunday. After worship she took his arm and led him downstairs to coffee hour and introduced him to her friends.

In the weeks prior to Sam's entering the church he had gone through a series of personal tragedies: his sister died of cancer, then his mother; later his wife left him. Sam was at the bottom. He remembered attending Sunday school when he was a child. He came back to a church.

The pastor visited with Sam and listened to his story; but the people who turned Sam's life around were Thelma and the women's group. Sam became their project. First he needed new clothes; they went through their hus-

bands' unused Christmas gifts and Sam had new clothes.
Sam was thin; he was not eating well. The women's group
took care of that, too. Members of the group invited him
over to their homes for supper. Every Sunday along with a
bag full of clean clothes there were casseroles and bis-
cuits. The word got around that Sam was a carpenter; the
women living in the senior citizen's housing complex told
the manager who was looking for a part-time handyman
about Sam's skills. He got the job.

Sam's life began to come together. Sam took an active
role in the adult Bible study class. He was asked to lead a
class; then he offered to be a lay reader in worship. The
pastor encouraged him to do volunteer work for a local
chapter of Habitat for Humanity. Working with Habitat,
Sam met families who were as discouraged as he had
been and he invited them to church. Sam has discovered a
calling, ministry through carpentry. But every Sunday
morning, Sam can be found sitting in worship among the
women who ministered to him. The congregation affec-
tionately refers to the women as "Sam's Angels."

It would have been simple for this small congregation to ig-
nore Sam when he entered the sanctuary one Sunday morning. But they didn't. One woman had the spiritual presence
to know that this young man needed her care. The pastor of
the church had a role in listening to Sam talk through his life.
But what Sam needed more was the love of women's group,
and he got it.

The new mission field we have been describing in this chapter are people like Sam Samuelson. Our communities are
filled with people who are deeply hurting and alone. How do
we respond to them? We believe that it is our small churches,
every one of them with saints like Thelma, which can minister to hurting people. It should be our mission to make our
spiritual presence an available gift to those who need it so
badly.

Visitation as Spiritual Presence

Ask any small church pulpit search committee what is their
highest priority for calling a minister, and they will respond,

VISIT. Why is it, then, that ministers view calling upon the membership and the people of the community as such a burden? Visiting can be the front line of mission in the small church. Getting out to homes, places of employment, sitting at a lunch counter and drinking coffee with the local police, are all powerful ways to share faith with people and to find out what is happening around town. For the small church to be engaged in mission, the pastor and people need to be calling and visiting people in the community.

The power of pastoral calling has been described in Conrad Richter's novel *A Simple, Honorable Man*. In this memorable scene, the Rev. Harry Donner, pastor of a small church in a Pennsylvania coal mining community, is visiting old friends—Mike Barrett, who is dying of black lung, and his wife Sally. A group of miners stand outside the house. Harry Donner has known the miners living in this isolated community for years, from his former work as owner of a general store.

"How's Mike?" Preacher Donner asked.

The men shook their heads.

"Not so good, Reverend," Jim Doran said. "The women are fanning him for breath now."

He could hear Mike breathing when he got to the door. It almost struck him in the face, a loud whistling and wheezing that shouldn't come from a human being. And could that be Mike Barrett himself, propped up in bed in the little parlor behind the storeroom, a wreck of a man wasted away to his bones, frail and transparent as glass, his hair turned to a tarnished silver? It was a shock to remember him as he used to be, filled with life and the devil.

Sally saw Harry Donner from the kitchen and came hurrying in to shake his hand. The look of thanks in her eyes was reward enough for missing Sunday school and walking six miles up the mountain. . . . Now she showed him her youngest girl and led him over to the bed.

"Harry Donner, me lad!" Mike Barrett greeted him faintly. "How'd they ever get a black coat on you, man?" Talking as little as that made him choke and cough till he brought up some thick black stuff which he spat in the can Sally held for him. . . .

At the end there was nothing to do but come around to it. Harry Donner laid his hand on the sick man's shoulder.

"I'd like to baptize you while I'm here, Mike," he said.

"You mean Sally'd like it!" Mike jeered.

"Well, of course she would. But I'm your friend and I'd like it, too. Will you let me do it for you?"

Mike sat there fighting the idea and fighting himself for fighting it.

"If Sally wants it, go ahead," he brought out at last.

Harry Donner took the Ministerial Acts from his pocket. . . . The men withdrew to the storeroom door and around the bed it became quiet except for the breathing. Harry Donner opened the book and his voice came out strong with life in the sickroom.

After the baptism Sally turned to the preacher, "Can he take Communion now, Reverend?"

"If he wants it," Harry Donner asked. "We won't push him. He doesn't need to take it if he doesn't want to."

The eyes of the bloodless miner were like pieces of coal. He seemed curiously calmed by the service and unaware of the terrible sucking and whistling sounds from his own chest. He motioned for the others to leave. . . .

The words and heart of the Eucharist ceremony had never seemed so rich and moving or yet so mysterious and inscrutable as when he repeated them today to this dying miner propped up in his unpainted Company house on Broad Mountain. . . .

At the end Harry Donner closed the little black book.

"That prayer was printed in here, Mike. Now I'd like to pray one of my own for you, if you want me to." He knelt by the bed and knotted his hands on the covers. He did not need to think what to say. Words of entreaty and intercession, as seldom came to him in his Mahanoy church flooded the room.

When he left, Sally tried to press a bill on him. He pushed it back.

"You need it for yourself, Sally."

"But I want you to come again, Reverend." He thought he knew what she meant.

"Any time," he told her.

"I'll never forget what you've done for us. It's the first time a minister's been in our house since your wife's father used to come and see us. . . .

The truth was, he told himself, that she had done more for him than he for her. It was her summons that had led him here, had let him bring God's word and sacrament to an old friend in his last bitter hours. Moreover, she had opened his eyes to this field of destitution and need lying unseen almost under his nose. . . .

When he stepped outside the men were still there, flanked now by some women and children. He sensed a respect he had never felt when out with the store team. Warmly he shook hands with them all. Several asked him if he would stop in at their houses to see them.[6]

Harry Donner brings a deep spiritual presence into the house of the dying coal miner Mike Barrett. What is moving about this scene is Donner's willingness to go to Mike's bedside and sit with him. Through his acceptance and care of Mike and Sally, Harry Donner earns the respect of the other miners. The spiritual presence embodied in Donner's compassion becomes mission when Richter writes, "Several asked him if he would stop at their houses to see them." A previously unidentified mission field opens up to the Reverend Harry Donner. Visiting people where they live and work in our communities is a powerful tool for doing mission.

We have described three ways in which the spiritual presence of a congregation is embodied in mission, through prayer, caring, and visiting. These examples in no way exhaust the possibilities. Do not overlook the mission that your church does simply through its spiritual presence in the community.

Mission as Public Presence

Jesus had a very public ministry. Every aspect of Jesus' ministry—preaching, teaching, healing, working miracles—took place in public forums in village centers, lakesides, homes.

People were attracted to Jesus or outraged by him through what they saw him do and heard him say. Everything Jesus did was out in the open for people to witness. Jesus' public ministry was a parable demonstrating our basic unity and interdependence with one another.

Mission as public presence is the way the church overcomes brokenness and fragmentation by modeling Jesus' vision of interdependence. Bringing people together is a critically important mission for the small church. In his book *The Company of Strangers*, Parker Palmer writes:

> We have all but lost the vision of the public. More than ever we need the process of public life to renew our sense of belonging to one another. But in our time, along with the loss of vision, opportunities for public interaction have also dwindled. We lack the facilities, the occasions, the hospitable spaces in which the public might come together to find and celebrate itself.[7]

And concerning the small church in particular, Palmer continues:

> The small church is an ideal setting with ample "facilities, occasions and hospitable spaces" to renew the "vision of the public." Worship services, weddings, funerals, public suppers, church fairs, community forums are all opportunities for our churches to model how people can come together and experience ourselves as a public. In such a life, strangers come in daily contact, grow accustomed to each other, learn to solve the problems which the common life poses, enrich and expand each other's lives. . . . It is a process which bring us out of ourselves into an awareness of our connectedness. . . .[8]

Opportunities for mission in creating a public life abound in the small church. We will consider three that are readily available: *public worship, affirming community,* and *advocacy.*

Public Worship

I begin at the heart of the congregation's life, with the act of worship. To be more precise, I mean "public worship," for corporate praise of God is meant to be a public, not a private act.[9]

Parker Palmer writes that "public worship" is anything but public: "Today, our worship is public only in the sense that anyone may enter the sanctuary on Sunday morning and join with us." The thought of the church worshiping in public places is frightening to many of us. Palmer is helpful when he suggests:

> If a public is to discover and sustain itself, our deepest symbols of unity, of brokenness, and of longing for reconciliation must be shared. That is the nature of worship—a symbolic celebration of the unity we have, a petition for forgiveness of the ways we have broken our bond, and a receptivity to the wholeness that is promised by God.[10]

What are some of the ways in which our worship can become public worship?

One of the most powerful public witnesses of "the brokenness and of longing for reconciliation" occurs every Good Friday when the churches of our community sponsor a "Stations of the Cross" worship service. The three-hour service is held in several downtown churches, but the power of the service takes place in between stops to participating churches, when a large, rough, and heavy wooden cross is dragged by worshipers down Main Street. Shoppers and merchants peer out of store windows at the unexpected sight of one hundred people following a cross shouldered by a few people. The scene as the cross slowly makes its way through the normal business traffic of the afternoon is a powerful reminder of the cost of Easter.

In another rural community, one congregation revived the Anglican tradition of Rogation Sunday. On a Sunday morning in springtime, during planting season, the priest blessed large sacks of seeds brought in by local farmers. After the service, the children paraded through the village carrying banners and leading prize cows and pigs. The message was clear: God is the creator and sustainer of all life.

Another way to make public worship public is simply to move the entire worship service outdoors to a local park or square. One congregation we know invites the community to worship by hosting "preaching dialogues" where well-known people are invited to share their spiritual journeys. The possibilities are endless.

Parker Palmer notes that we are so cautious about trampling on the well-established boundary between church and state that we have "banished religious symbolism from the public realm." What has taken the place of religious symbolism in the public realm are symbols of consumerism, "buying and selling, having and owning, consuming and competing for more." The mission of the small church in public presence is helping to renew public life by making what we value more visible. Palmer issues the church a challenge, "Do we have the imagination to pronounce the promise of unity and the healing of wounds?"[11]

Affirming Community

People in our society tend to live in isolation from one another. The life of the small church is characterized by numerous ways in which people come together to affirm their common life. Among the activities that make up much of our corporate life (and that we often take for granted) are church suppers, fairs, bazaars, weddings, and funerals. These are wonderful ways to bring people together who otherwise would not know one another. Parker Palmer describes the importance of the potluck supper for an urban congregation:

> I once asked a politically active black minister in Washington, D.C., to name the primary task in his ministry. I suppose I expected him to say something about political organizing, protest and the like. Instead he said, "To provide my people with a rich social life." I asked, "Do you mean parties and potlucks and socials and things like that?" thinking his answer sounded a bit frivolous. "Of course," he said, "things like that give my people the strength to struggle in public."[12]

In our community, church suppers are called "public suppers" because a cross-section of the town attends. One of the women who has helped host these public suppers for forty years has the job of seating people in the crowded church basement. Her gift is to seat people who have never met next to each other. She clearly understands what she calls her "ministry of introductions." In a not-so-small way, this woman helps overcome the suspicion between "natives" and "out-of-towners."

There are countless ways in which the small church can affirm the life of the community. Funeral services can be opportunities to lift up the lives of "the saints" and to share common historical values. Wedding services can be celebrations of family life and the undergirding support of the wider community. In a world in which people are increasingly isolated from one another and are feeling powerless and desperate, there can be no more important mission for the church than to reconnect people with one another and their spiritual roots. If you see a church public supper as simply a fundraising event, look again.

Advocacy

Small churches are grassroots organizations that know what is going on in their community. In public worship people offer prayers for neighbors who are unemployed because a factory shuts down. Mission as advocacy means giving voice to issues and concerns in the community. Your church can be an advocate for abused children and people who are unemployed. Churches are ideal locations to hold meetings where community groups can discuss problems. Pulpits have traditionally been places where the biblical mandate for justice has been proclaimed.

Carol Bly's book *Letters from the Country* is filled with practical examples of how churches can take on the role as community advocate. She suggests that churches can take a leading role by holding public forums designed to debate local controversial topics.

I propose that small community groups develop panels for
Enemy Evenings. Obviously some much better word has to
be used. . . . Enemy Evenings would definitely need two
things: a firm master of ceremonies in whom general affection for human beings would be paramount . . . second, it
would need very just panel representation.

Here is a suggested subject: The growth of shopping
malls around small towns.

Suggested participants: local promoters of comprehensive plans; Main Street businessmen; members of senior
citizen's clubs; high school Ecology Club members; the
mayor or council members. . . .

A painful fact of American life is that people from small
towns are afraid of directness. . . . I commend frank panel
evenings with opponents taking part; let's try that for a
change of air, after years of chill and evasive tact.[13]

In our rural community, comprehensive planning was mandated by the state. People were angrily divided on the topic,
but nowhere were people with opposing views sitting down
to talk. Picking up on Carol Bly's suggestion that churches
host "Enemy Evenings" (we didn't call them that), our
church hosted a series of evening informational forums. For
the first time advocates of growth and no-growth, zoning and
no-zoning presented their views and listened to one another.
The purpose is to create a public life, to enhance the level of
discourse, and to get people talking to one another about
things that matter. The ground rule we set before the forum
was that people were encouraged to argue, but that we had to
leave as friends.

On occasion, the church is called to take a clear stand on a
community issue. The following story describes how a small
congregation advocated for children's health care.

Late on Easter Sunday, I received a telephone call from the
hospital emergency room. The quiet voice of an ex-
hausted physician told me that a twelve-year-old girl had
died. The cause of death was preventable if only the child
had been treated earlier. The death was needless. The

child's parents were poor farmers and had neither health insurance nor the money to pay for a visit to the doctor's office.

A day later the doctor told me about the growing number of families in the community who had no money for medical care and were not being treated. The tragedy would be repeated again and again if something was not done to make health care available to the ''newly poor families.''

Because our small church had a history of advocating for the needs of low-income people, the physician called me asking for help. ''We need to set up a free clinic for children.'' I called a meeting at our church bringing together doctors, area health agencies, social workers, and the ecumenical church community. Everybody around the table shared the common concern about children at risk. We needed to act immediately to prevent another tragedy. In a matter of weeks three well-child clinics were organized to serve the needs of children of working poor parents in our large rural county.

The role of the church community in organizing the well-child clinics was primarily as an advocate for children. The church challenged the complacent attitude that everyone had access to quality health care. Meeting together at a church, people who had never talked to one another before came together to meet a need. The only cost to the Christian community was speaking out on a controversial topic. The pay-off to the churches was priceless in the good will it generated in the community at-large, and especially in the eyes of the working poor who came to see the church as a friend and advocate.

We believe that one of the worst things that can be said about a church is that it is boring. Congregations that affirm community, or advocate on behalf of those without a voice become identified by the community for their public stand. "You're the church that hosted the rally protesting sexual assault. . . ." "You're the church that planned the 'old home days' weekend. . . ." "You're the church that spoke out against the plant closing. . . ." All of these are examples of the church in mission and signs of hope both for the church and its community.

Conclusion

The Southern civil rights marches of the 1960s were not so much political demonstrations as they were a spiritual movement. The leadership came out of the churches. Before the marchers took to the streets, they gathered in churches to worship God. Martin Luther King, Jr., led people in prayer, joined in singing traditional spirituals, and preached the Word of God to them. Worship gave the civil rights demonstrators the clear spiritual grounding that sent them into the streets.

Mission begins with prayer. The life of prayer will lead us into mission. Despite our frequent attempts to use prayer as an escape from the world, the God we meet in prayer connects us to one another as a church and as part of the world. In prayer we return to the center, to Christ, and there we are refreshed, reconnected with others, and sent into the world. Spiritual presence discovered through prayer and worship is the foundation for all mission.[14]

As you seek to lead your church into local mission, return to the center of prayer, study, and worship.

Strategies for Implementation

The emerging focus for mission is the local congregation.

If the mission field is now the local community, we need to learn how to "equip the saints for the work of ministry" (Ephesians 4:12). To prepare for the new mission frontier we first need to describe the life of the congregation, for describing what we are already doing in our church helps us understand the gifts that we bring to mission. Remember that the key to doing local mission is discovering your congregation's unique gifts.

Here are some steps to follow as you begin to discover the mission that is your congregation's calling, the work of ministry.

1. Describe the *program, process, context,* and *identity* of your congregation.[15]

2. Define the ways your congregation is active in mission by its presence in the community. Use the categories *Symbolic Presence, Spiritual Presence,* and *Public Presence* to help identify on-going mission.

3. What new ideas and insights does your study suggest for ways to broaden the mission of your congregation?

4. Write a mission statement that describes the particular gifts of your congregation and how those gifts are expressed in local mission. Be as specific as possible.

Chapter 3

Small-Church Mission: People

Making Mission Personal

I do not know how one gets to be a "church researcher," but it seems as though it would be a fun job, running around with a spiritual thermometer, taking the temperature of the church, maybe hoping for an outbreak of fever here and there, but dreading the awful, too-frequent reading of chronic hypothermia.

Well, one such researcher looked at evangelism in the local church, and concluded that, as we all suspected, some local churches do evangelism well, with energy and enthusiasm and some degree of effectiveness, while others don't. Secondly, the researcher found that some congregations have formally designated evangelism committees, and some don't. Again, not much of a surprise there. But the researcher also discovered that if there is a correlation between those churches that do evangelism well and those that have evangelism committees, the correlation is a negative one! In plain English, churches that are good evangelists go about it spontaneously, personally, and informally. Those that have to organize a formal committee to get the job done, tend not to get the job done.

Now a particular small church may or may not do evangelism well, but small churches in general would certainly understand that the energy involved in organizing a committee is that much less energy available to do the work. The goal in small churches is not committees and structures and organizations, but relationships. When things go right in the small church, they go right at the personal level and no impersonal organization or structure can compensate for the personal. The small church lives and moves and has its being in a world of persons and relationships. One of the great missions of the small church is to keep this world alive, offering a bit of leaven (and heaven) to a society that is bent on programming, institutionalizing, and depersonalizing. Of course, programs, institutions, and impersonal approaches have their place, but if they are to be used in the small church they must be "managed" as alien methodologies. The personal approach is the natural approach in small churches. So the one who would increase mission effectiveness in a small church needs to be familiar and comfortable with the personal nature of the small-church culture.

The Personal Nature of Small-Church Mission: An Example

Consider this story as an illustration of the "personal" way mission is done in small churches. This is a true story. I know: I was there.

> It was a Sunday morning in September. A visitor to our church stood during sharing time in worship ("sharing time" is a structure we have both to celebrate and live out the personal nature of small-church worship) and announced that he was "John Lydgate, Bill's son." That was an interesting and appropriate introduction. John was a stranger to us, so although he was in his fifties, the best way he could make himself known to us was to name his father, to cite his lineage, to remind us of the people from whom he had come. And being connected to Bill, to whom we were connected, gave him a connection to us.
>
> John's father, Bill, now in his eighties, was the grandson of early missionaries to the Hawaiian Islands. And Bill, though now retired in New York state, twenty years before had "saved" the church. That story goes like this. Rev.

Stan Pratt had become pastor of the Harbor Church on Block Island in 1971. In order to engender some new life in the faithful few, he had created a youth group, and was taking a car full of kids to a play on the mainland when he was struck by a hit-and-run driver. He spent weeks in the hospital and the better part of the year out of commission. Two deacons stepped forward to keep worship going and the congregation meeting. Neither had any seminary training or any particular biblical expertise, yet week after week after week they alternated leadership in the pulpit. Nobody now remembers all the deacons said, but everyone remembers with appreciation and affection that they kept the church functioning in a very dark hour. One of those two deacons was Bill Lydgate.

So when John identified himself as Bill's son, he had an instant place in our family and instant credibility. It turned out that John had joined the Peace Corps in the sixties and had traveled the globe since, and when he went on to say that he and his wife, Charlotte, had been doing missionary work with the Church of South India, well, we weren't surprised! (According to small- church/small-town theology, the apple does not fall far from the tree!) Someone has remarked that God has no grandchildren, meaning we each need to arrive at personal faith in Jesus Christ. We know that, but we also know "that the Lord your God is God; he is the faithful God, keeping his covenant of love to a thousand generations of those who love him and keep his commands" (Deuteronomy 7:9).

John described their work in economic development, creating jobs and self-sufficiency and respect among the Indian farmers. Then he thanked us for allowing him to worship and share with us, and sat down.

Immediately Matilda stood up. Matilda is not only a person; she is a character. She struggles with a malady caused by and causing emotional distress. She has been hospitalized a dozen times. She has a heart of gold, but frequently throws sand not oil, and an occasional monkey wrench, too, into the gears of human relationships. We love Matilda but we give her a wide berth. But now Matilda stood up. Gulp, I thought.

"Well, I'm sure John could use some help. Let's take up a collection!" said Matilda.

Double gulp, I thought, moisture appearing on my brow. Everyone knows some things in church life are sacred, and right at the top of the list is THE COLLECTION. We can't just add a collection because Matilda says so, no matter how credible Bill's son is to us.

"John, our deacons are meeting on Thursday night," I said quickly. "Can you come to the meeting? We can talk over the best way we can support your mission."

John nodded agreement. Matilda smiled success. Beads of sweat dripped down my face.

Thursday night came, and the deacons listened with great interest to all the details of John's work — sera culture, the provision of the silkworms, the trees, harvesting, storage, marketing. "But," said John, "what I really need help with is in another village."

And then John went on to share about the dream of the South Indian Church to start a technical institute where women could learn to type and sew, and earn wages with which to buy the necessities of life.

"What could you use?"

"Five sewing machines would get us started."

"How much?" asked our ever practical deacons.

"$100 to $120 each."

"Move we set a goal of $600."

"Second."

"All in favor?"

"O.K. It's unanimous. What's next, Pastor?"

All of this went on while I sat in stunned silence. Finally I found my voice. "Where's this $600 to come from?"

"Why, we'll pass the plate. Get the word out. It'll come, you'll see."

And it did! Over the next few weeks the money appeared. Some families "bought" one sewing machine each. Some threw a few extra bucks in the plate. We even received a check in the mail from a townsperson who had never worshiped with us, but somehow got caught up in the excitement.

When the dust finally settled we had raised enough money to buy *seven* sewing machines and a haystack-full of needles, too! How thrilling it was one year later, when John and Charlotte arrived back on Block Island with a personal thank-you from the Bishop of South India, photographs of the new sewing machines and the beaming faces of the first graduating class of seamstresses.

We had been touched by John's personal presence and appeal to us. We had reached out and touched the lives of a handful of people in India. And in time our hearts were touched with the warmth and the joy of Christ's Spirit.

God's end was to make the Kingdom just a bit more real. God's means was the personal: Matilda and her wild ideas; John and his presence, tangibly in our midst; Bill and his selfless devotion to keep a small, struggling church open, receiving one fruit from his labor, twenty years later.

People are the pieces of the small-church mission puzzle. Institutionalized programs, no matter how skillfully done or how theologically correct, just won't have the same results in the small church.

I relearned this truth while John was with us, for at the same time we were publicizing the World Mission Offering. It was a generalized, denominational appeal to do the same kind of ministry that John and Charlotte represented in person. Our mission committee duly promoted the appeal, and we received a very good offering for us—$211, a little more than usual. The offering for John and his work, however, was over $900, more than four times our response to the organized but distant world mission collection. Small-church life is personal, so small-church people respond to the mission that is personal. It is consistent with our nature. And, as the Incarnation demonstrates, it is also God's preferred way of doing mission.

The Enterprise of Personal Mission

So enamored was Archimedes of the lever that he claimed, "Give me a place to stand, and I will move the earth."[1] As Christians we, too, are called to be "earth-movers." The people of Thessalonica rightly accused Paul and the early

Christians of having "turned the world upside down" (Acts 17:6). That's what Christian mission is all about: moving our world, moving it closer to God's intention for it.

But, like Archimedes, we need a place to stand and a lever. In the small church we stand squarely in a personal world. We understand why the Incarnate One was named Immanuel, God-with-us, for God had to be with us *as a person* to be with *us* at all. We understand why the genealogies are so important to Matthew and Luke, because until we know someone's family connections, we can't place them in our peopled world. We live as persons in a God-created cosmos of personalness. It is in those realities that we understand redemption, salvation, and mission. The personal is our world. This is where we stand.

And this is our lever, too. Our means of moving toward greater involvement in the mission of God is the personal dimension of small-church dynamics. At first glance it may seem that if the small church's way of doing mission is for individuals to minister to other individuals in a personal way, then two dynamics are essential: persuasion and modeling. Preach and practice what you preach, and if others are faithful they will follow. If the pacesetters in a small church are not actively involved in ministering to others in Christ's name and in proclaiming our vocation as Christ's servants, then the pace-followers won't be either.

But there is a more powerful dynamic than either persuasion or modeling, and that is the personal nature of small-church culture itself. The small church as a sociological entity has a certain personal way of doing things that can be distinguished from the programmatic and institutional ways of doing things.

Personal, Not Programmatic

For mission to be done programmatically, at least four functions must be accomplished by the missioner: a goal must be set; a plan must be adopted; resources must be marshalled and allocated; and measurements must be taken. These four procedures assure that the programmatic approach is a very productive way of operating. Because of the high productivity of this approach, it is used by business, taught in seminaries, and has come to be considered the normal, "right" way of doing things. Thus programming takes on a primacy in theory that it does not have in real, face-to-face communities.

In our society the programming approach has become the dominant way of doing mission. Yet in the small church, a square personal peg shouldn't be pounded into a round program hole, even when the square personals are judged by the round programmers to be unresponsive, unskilled obstructionists. While there is sometimes truth in these assessments, the mismatch is usually more a matter of the social system and the culture of the small church. The programmatic approach is just not natural for small-church people.

The personal approach uses responsiveness more than planning. All Christians pray, "Your Kingdom come." The distinguishing question is, How is the Kingdom seen as coming? For the programmatic Christian, the Kingdom is to be realized, at least in part, through the future-oriented, linear-sequential organizing ability of the planner, inspired by the Holy Spirit. For the personal Christian, the Kingdom is coming through God's direct initiative. We have but to respond to God's call in the circumstances and opportunities of life. The personal approach, then, does not have so much to do with planning as with coordinating with God's unfolding plan.

The following story shows the differences between the personal and programmatic approaches to mission revealed in an investigation into the process by which some American Baptist churches became racially integrated.

Nobody integrates willingly.

At least, that's the impression many Americans have. A glance at some of the integration moves of the last two decades offers some hints as to why many Americans think integration has to be forced on us.

Not long ago, American public schools across the land were forced by federal court mandates to desegregate. Public institutions were told their funds would be withheld if they did not comply with affirmative-action hiring quotas. Countless neighborhoods were faced with a choice between open housing demands or endless lawsuits. As a result, many Americans formed an opinion of how integration was accomplished. It had to be planned, enforced, and regulated. It certainly didn't just "happen," or so it seemed. But it wasn't always that way. Throughout the country, in quiet ways that seldom made headlines, integration began to happen. We now call it "racial/ethnic inclusiveness." And it works. Even so, five pastors from Connecticut to California say integration in their churches was neither planned nor anticipated. But God—and a handful of God's faithful servants—made it happen.

This might be an untold story: that churches, and American Baptist churches in particular, became integrated for no particular reason, and actually quite by chance.

If there is a common thread winding through the history of those congregations that model inclusiveness, it seems to be this: it just happened. There's a low-key tone to these developments. No marches. No demonstrations. No intentionality. Just people looking for a church, and other people who welcomed them. Then there were mutual struggles to get to know and love one another, and God blessed the results.

The guiding insight is that long-range planning—valuable as it is—is not the total answer to all the problems the church faces. No one could have sat down to plan a comprehensive strategy for integrating the congregation or for making it more inclusive.

"Long-range planning is only good up to a point," Gene Bartlett said long ago. In the end, a pastor and a congregation simply have to "be open to the winds of God."

When that happens, the beloved community of God—richly varied and warmly inclusive—begins to happen. No marches, no demonstrations, no lawsuits or court orders. Just a quiet miracle.[2]

While the programmatic approach focuses on a goal and describes it with a mission statement, the personal approach is energized to "right" things. This "righting" of things occurs on three levels. The first is a desire to see God's righteousness prevail. This is incarnated in many ways, from concern for the recovery of an alcoholic to agitation for a fairer farm policy.

The second level could be imaged in the righting of a ship that has been listing. Most small-church people intuitively see life as a leaking ship. God has given each of us the capacity to bail, and as long as we are bailing as fast as the ship is leaking, life stays in balance. But sometimes the weight shifts—an illness or death, unemployment or low commodity prices, discouragement or disgruntlement strikes. So the ship lists and then even small waves threaten to swamp it. But through the personal presence of Christian brothers and sisters, the weight can be redistributed, the ship righted, and bailing resumed.

The third level of "righting" occurs when something that was right ceases to be right. A long-term member drops out, a case of child molestation surfaces, the impersonal and so inaudible cries of the disadvantaged in India start ringing in our ears through the presence of a John Lydgate, some of our "best" farmers go bankrupt, drugs start to infiltrate our schools—when we register *these* things, things are no longer right. The dissonance between the way things should be and the way they are releases energy. This energy can go into lament and victimization, or it can go into mission and action. But the "righting" of things that have gone wrong is the goal of the personal approach.

The programmatic approach recruits, organizes, and deploys resources. The personal approach does not have (or does not understand that it has) the same extent of resources. It sees what it has in personal terms, and so it gives of itself. A shoulder to cry on, a helping hand, a kick in the pants, a listening ear. What it has to give is its own presence, a standing by. So its key is not organizational ability but compassion.

The personal approach utilizes its existing social life and social structures to carry its mission. The little Baptist church in Rome, Maine, describes how they go about extending Christ's welcome in this way:

The Church Inviting

At 9:00 A.M. each Wednesday morning, church women gather for Bible study and discussion, after which they call on new families and shut-ins.

The programmatic approach knows success when its output equals or exceeds its target indices. A "home for the homeless" program that aims to house fifty percent of the homeless in its city and actually houses fifty-eight percent knows success—at least until it redefines its goal at seventy-five percent. On the other hand, the personal approach knows success subjectively: when things feel "right" again, God has been here.

Although many small churches will and should use programmatic elements in their mission endeavors, this approach is not usually the best way to move toward greater outreach effort in a small church. A better strategy will include responding to God's call in particular needs, realizing that what we really have to offer is not so much our coin as it is our *koinonia*, channeling the energy that is released when things aren't right, and remembering that in the small church the world is judged by measures of the heart.

Personal, Not Institutional

A second distinction regarding the way in which mission is done in the small church is that it is not bureaucratic or institutional. Clearly, a society as large as ours could not function without complex administrative structures and institutions. Two hundred fifty million people could not operate on a face-to-face basis. Institutions such as governmental agencies, large corporations, and our educational and health care delivery systems have certain functions and structures in common: namely, they are bureaucratic. This is not necessarily pejorative; it simply means they function by means of bureaus. That is, they break reality into slices and categories and deal with things in that way, not holistically.

Institutions function hierarchically as well as bureaucratically, in an up-down orientation to life and relationships. "Let me speak to your supervisor," is often the best way to cut the gordian knot of bureaucratic red tape. On the other hand, "My superiors will never buy that" is a very functional way of saying no without getting personal. On two separate occasions I have dealt with two different departments of the State of Rhode Island. In both cases, once on behalf of my church, once on behalf of a local nonprofit group, my organization was put through the wringer of very technical conformity to rules in order to obtain a permit. Every protest or appeal for reason was met with, "Well, you can always take your chances with our Board." Gulp. Not THE BOARD. Finally, though, we pushed through and made our appeal to the Board, and amazingly, we found them to be very open and reasonable. The invocation of the authority of the board demonstrates the hierarchy of power in the institution, where nobody wants to take personal responsibility without hiding behind the powers above.

Finally, institutions are impersonal as well as bureaucratic and hierarchical. In fact, they deliberately seek to be impersonal in order to be impartial. They work on the basis of abstract principles that become incarnated not in people, but in policies and procedures, and on this basis they remake the world. In social service jargon, for example, people are not cared for; rather, clients are serviced and depersonalized into caseloads. Their humanity is abstracted away, so that the institution can deal with them on its own terms. In the programmatic approach, programs take on a reality into which people are then fitted. Institutions go even further. They take on a longevity born of inertia. They are "peopled" by professional roles. And only at this third level of abstraction are the roles filled with people.

So you can see why small-church people, living in a personal world, are hard put to feel at home in an institution or to organize anything institutionally. Small-church people are not institutional. They do not compartmentalize life, but try to live holistically. Although there certainly is a pecking order in all face-to-face societies, there is a far greater degree of egalitarianism, too. Personal authority is the authority of small-church people. Life, and mission as a part of life, is approached on a case-by-case basis. Every situation is different, since every person is coming from a different place. No abstract principle can deal as effectively with the living of life as does the tailoring to the personal realities of the face-to-face society.

The institutional approach is thus very foreign to small-church people. While the programmatic can be adapted and hybridized in the small church, the institutional approach requires a major shift from small-church values and ways of operating. And yet when they have to, many face-to-face societies learn how to deal with institutions. I remember being escorted through the Hopi Tribal offices on their reservation in northern Arizona. The building was neat and attractive, the people friendly and helpful, but I remember most clearly the room in which entire walls from floor to ceiling were lined with the legislative record of the U.S. Congress. This relatively small tribe of about ten thousand people knew that the most significant feature of their environment was not the San Francisco Peaks or the Mesas or even the ongoing disputes with the Navajos over land rights. The most significant feature of their environment was the institution called the U.S. Government, and they had organized themselves to be informed and active relative to that institution. So, too, many small churches, small townships, and urban neighborhoods have come to learn the ways of the institutions that shape their lives in order that they might have an impact on them and move them toward righteousness. This is not an easy mission for a small church, but it is one that many have taken on.

If institutions are the way in which complex, modern societies function, then how does a small, face-to-face society function? It functions through its culture, through the sum of the ecology, the behaviors (both individual and patterned), the artifacts and symbols, and the ways in which these symbols are articulated and conceptualized by a self-identified people. And people are the doers, the incarnation of their own culture.

The culture is the context in which our humanity is shaped. So our discussion of the personal nature of mission in the small church would be incomplete and shallow if we were not to also lift up the cultural dimension. Unless small-church culture is understood, its personal nature cannot be appreciated or utilized effectively for Christ's mission.

The culture of a small church is "the way we do things around here." Mission needs to become "the way we do things around here" if a small church desires to be healthy and faithful. Those who would enhance Christ's mission in a small church must not simply aim to do one more mission project, program, or activity, although this may be a worthwhile short-term goal. The final aim must be to become a mission people, a people who register need in the community around them, a people who respond with the heart of Christ, a people who believe that even a cup of cold water has value in eternity and so never disparages "little" ministries, a people who will not settle for becoming a better body of Christ unless that also includes making the Kingdom more real in the place in which they are planted.

Many a mission effort has been pushed through small churches by a well-meaning pastor or new church member. (I know: I have ramrodded my share.) Yet when the dust settled, the church was no more "mission oriented" than it was before the effort. Small-church mission is not good enough if it is simply an aberrant activity generated by an occasional outburst of energy and/or guilt. Mission must become part of the very culture of the small church, part of the way small-church people see the world, live in it, and make sense of it.

Bill Briggs advocates a certain kind of mission activity that will change the missioners as well as the missionees. In his book *Faith Through Works* he shares a process for involving people personally in the need and the lives of the recipients. His strategy for changing the culture of a small church is through personal contact with others, a strategy fully harmonious with the nature of the small church.

Any mission activity that so exhausts a small congregation that it requires months to recover will certainly change the culture of that congregation, but unfortunately, it will also move it away from future mission activity. Do-able, short-term, success-engendering mission activities are strategically wise moves for building a mission orientation into the culture of a small church.

John Dorean pastors a small church in western Pennsylvania. Listen to him as he reflects on the changes in culture ("the way we do things around here") that have resulted from a patient, incrementally developed housing mission.

"Why, Daddy? Why can't everyone have a house?" That was the question posed to our senior high youth group leader by his four-year-old daughter. He had been with eleven folks from the church building low-cost affordable homes for the poor as part of the 1990 Jimmy Carter Work Project. As he tried to explain to his family where he had been and what he'd been doing, talking about the destitute conditions that many of the world's people live in, that was the question that she kept coming back to. It is a question that I hope will haunt our church family and many others like ours as we seek to move out of the complacency of our American comfort and set about responding to the needs of God's people in need.

As the pastor of a small church for more than eight years now, I have long been excited about the power of hands-on missions to excite and motivate a congregation's interest and involvement in ministry. To be sure a whole lot of good, lasting things occur through ministries like Habitat: houses get built, families in need receive a helping hand, the Kingdom's concern for justice gets demonstrated. But even more exciting than that for me personally are the changes I see getting worked out in the lives of the volunteers themselves. And those changes become a veritable seed-bed for the transformation of the small church.

The adventure began. We are far from a wealthy church, located as we are in what social workers would label the fringes of Appalachia, a mining community with a high level of unemployment. So raising the money to fly our group to southern California on the way to our destination in Mexico was not an easy task. But car washes, pancake breakfasts, spaghetti dinners, slave days, and the like eventually got the job done. We also asked each of the participants to write ten fund-raising letters to folks outside of the church family asking for their support. A jug at the front of the church to gather everyone's loose pocket change also netted more than $500.

We decided that an experience of this sort could radically reshape our lives and even the life of the church for a long time to come.

We were not disappointed. Along with 1200 other volunteers, Jimmy and Rosalynn Carter among them, our group of eleven spent six days sleeping in two-person tents, showering with solar-heated two-gallon water bags, drinking bottled water, and growing not so fond of portable toilets. Rising at 5:00 A.M. every morning for breakfast and devotions, we began work shortly before seven and quit work around 5:30 every afternoon.

That's the kind of blisters and sweat stuff that kids remember for a long time but not the kind of thing that changes lives. But rolling out of the tent every morning to look across the valley to see the plywood shacks and utter desolation of the community of Matamoros, working side by side with the families of that community who would soon be the recipients of those homes, visiting in the evenings those same shacks of those same families and being welcomed as friends, that is the stuff that opens eyes and shapes perspectives and encourages transformed lives like almost nothing else.

Probably my favorite comment came from our youngest worker who challenged us all profoundly with the naked truth when she said, "When I am living in this country all I

want, all I think about is more and more and more. But that
week in Mexico showed me just how greedy that really is."

Now again, if those comments came from a missions
speaker or a visitor, the congregation might be impressed
momentarily and then forget about it. But when we are
talking about our own kids, our own friends and neighbors
sharing in that way, the impact is multiplied. The first Sunday we were back not less than eight members who had
heard the presentations left saying, "Where are we going
next year?"[3]

The Environment of Small-Church Mission

Small-church mission is a personal enterprise (of people,
for people, through the involvement, efforts, and presence of
people) because the small church is a personal reality.[4] But
small-church mission must also be a personal enterprise because of the environment in which it exists. Small churches
live in a personal environment, and in their mission they seek
to affect real people in the nitty gritty of their lives.

In his article *How Do Small Towns Work? A Guide for New Pastors*, Richard Griffin claims that many new, seminary-trained
pastors do a poor job of influencing their congregations toward greater faithfulness in mission because the pastors are
still living in the seminary's world of ideas, while small-
church people live in a world of political realities. (By
"politics" Griffin means the authority/power relationships
between persons, not national political parties in Washington, D.C.) This small-town world, Griffin says, is shaped by
the idolatrous god of "respectability" which ranks each person and family in the town, giving influence to some and de-
nying it wholesale to others.

This god also has three "persons," Griffin claims: Ownership, Community Support, and Local History. Thus, Ownership makes the landowners far more powerful, present, and
"really there" than laborers, who are far more likely to leave
the community. This power is accorded regardless of personal
abilities and "rightness" on any particular issues. (I remember the upsurge in the personal effectiveness of my ministry

on Block Island when it became known that I had purchased property and was building a house!) Community Support—ranging from holding local office (high) to keeping your lawn mowed (minimal)—conveys personal power to the individual in the community. And Local History provides a pecking order of personal power, starting with several generations of filial presence and wending its way down through "married into the family," "grew up here and left, but came back," and so on. (I remember one parishioner complaining about an adult child of another parishioner claiming to BE a Block Islander when "that family only moved to the island in 1816"!)

Obviously these categories contain many subsets. And people interested in acquiring additional power and presence in such a community can attempt to make up in one category what is lacking in another. The net result is a variegated and changing landscape of personal power and influence, and this is the environment in which small churches find themselves seeking to do mission. The configuration of this environment of personal powers and positions is constantly changing, but the fundamental nature remains the same. Recent changes in rural demographics have undermined the power of Local History in many places, while Community Service has waxed as a source of personal power. Yet even in the city, where not so much is known of each person and family and institutional variables are of greater significance, it still remains the case that *what* you know is of much less significance than *who* you know! The environment in which a small church, rural or urban, seeks to do mission is still a personal environment.

Griffin concludes his article with four strategies for increasing faithfulness in such an environment:

> First, despite the possible distastefulness of the idea, a pastor working for change in the small church will have to work *politically*. Many of the writings on the small church describe to the reader the political process of change in the small church. The pastor must *not* attempt to work any other way. (That is, at least not organizationally. None of

this is meant in any way to exclude the possibility of change brought about by true revival!) The finest preaching in the world will not change the small church: all the pastor's preaching (presentation of truth) does is give him/her the right to enter the political process of the church.

Second, the change process in the small church is subject to the strengths and weaknesses of the political process. One of the strengths of this process is that if the pastor *can* effect change by working through the leaders of the church, that change is much more likely to be permanent. One of the weaknesses is that the pastor will probably be able to effect, at most, only *one* major change during his/her tenure. (There are some rare exceptions to this rule, but it is unwise to *plan* on being one of them.)

Third, the pastor should work on the most *basic* change needed. This is not always the most obvious or glaring deficiency in the church. But given that the pastor in a small town can probably effect only *one* major change, s/he should look for the root problem in the church and concentrate on that.

Fourth, once the pastor has targeted the area in which change is needed, s/he should work toward that change *alone*. The pastor may lay the groundwork for the next minister by mentioning all of the things s/he is concerned about. The pastor may speak about evangelism, mutual love, forgiving others, refraining from passing judgment—anything in which s/he sees a need. The pastor may even preach on these things so that the next minister isn't starting from scratch. But the pastor of the rural church needs to focus all his/her efforts toward *change* on effecting the most basic change his/her church needs to make.[5]

The Personal Effort of Small-Church Mission

I was sipping away during coffee hour one Sunday morning following worship when Kathy came over. Never having been accused of being shy, she launched right in to what was on her mind.

"Do ya know what I like about this church?" Well, now, that

was a question! "I'll tell you," she said gratuitously, as I managed to slip a "What" in edgewise. "I matter!"

"You matter," I reflected back in my best Rogerian tone.

"You're darn tootin' I matter. I am important. I make a difference here. I'm somebody. We're a small group, so if I decide to do anything it has an impact!"

I knew what Kathy had added to our church and to our community life. And I knew she was right. She did matter.

That small-church light has been hidden too long under a bushel. "How can one person fight city hall?" "We're such a small group. What could we do?" Such disempowering scripts are so close and yet so far. The premise is right, but the conclusion is wrong. "We are such a small group" is the great advantage of the small church, not its disadvantage. Once motivated, the small church can mobilize quickly. It doesn't need a two-month proposal review process before the mission committee, followed by a vote of the executive board, prior to a budgetary allocation from the finance board. In my church two phone calls will get the ball rolling. In our church's "culture" it is better to make a well-intentioned mistake than to bury our treasure. And since we use a zero-based budgeting approach (which for us simply means that we have zero budget to work with!), we are always in a "go" posture.

So, the premise "We are a small group" should lead to the conclusion "therefore, we can mobilize for ministry at the drop of a hat." If large churches and denominational allocations and ecumenical agencies are the "big guns" of Christ's church, then small churches are God's guerrillas! We can pop in, deliver evil a quick rabbit punch, and scoot out before the devil even knows we were there! The Kingdom isn't going to come through sheer numbers or economic power, but through the amazingly unquenchable personal presence of righteousness. It is only the individual who can fight evil. Committees can't do it. Armies can't do it. Congresses can't do it. Only the one, the person who is willing to give his or her life to right that wrong, can do it.

My spirit continually goes back to the story of David and Goliath. Not that I am into bloodshed, but I am continually in need of paradigms of victory. In this story God has given us one of the best. The whole army of Israel with its tall king Saul stands, actually cowers, far up on the hillside away from Goliath. The taunts of this enemy have left them paralyzed with fear. In the face of his might and arrogance and the size of his weapons, they are immobilized. Into this scene enters David. He hears the same words but registers them differently. The God of Israel being insulted and ridiculed—to him they are fighting words. And he looks out at the heavy, massively armed Goliath and thinks, not how overpowered I am, but rather, I can be in and out before he even says go! And that day the mighty warrior fell to a lean, quick bantamweight who was willing to take a risk for God.

Kathy is right. She does matter. Each and every person in a small church matters. Each and every one is in the strategic position to mount an attack against the evil around us. Kathy strode forth to meet her Goliath by accepting the chair of the local Chamber of Commerce, a group rife with hostility and division. At great personal cost to her own psychological well-being, she required meetings to be conducted with personal respect and politeness. She introduced times of prayer for reconciliation. She looked for new approaches. She paid for her efforts by being summarily voted out, but for one moment, brief here, long in heaven, the light shone.

All God needs is one person with a vision for righteousness, and a willingness to live into the vision. Sometimes one person's vision can change an entire town, as it did in Sewell, New Jersey.

> Ecological stewardship can "profit" a church. That's the story of Sewell Community Baptist Church of Sewell, New Jersey, and its glass recycling program. Our ministry began in the 1970s and continued into the 1980s. Its demise came as the result of the township's inability to continue transporting glass to the recycler and its own mandated commu-

nity recycling program. For almost a decade Sewell Baptist practiced a community witness in ecological stewardship.

We became involved because one person in the congregation also saw the program as a way to receive additional income for use within the church and community. About 15 to 20 members of the congregation were enlisted to sort and break the glass. We also secured metal drums for storage, purchased a shed and built a platform. At first the church was responsible for getting the glass to the recycling site. It was later picked up by the township. First it was only the church. Then the community became involved, saving glass and bringing it to the church. Some from the community volunteered to help with the project. The Sewell Community Baptist Church is the only church in a small town of 500 families.

As the program continued, we evaluated it in relation to the congregation's mission and ministry. In spite of problems, the project was successful. The church netted $750-$1250 per year. That created another problem: how to spend the income since most of the glass came from the community and the program was supported by community volunteers. After due consideration we determined that the funds accrued could not be used exclusively within the Sewell Church, but should benefit the wider community.

The congregation had a youth program that included non-church youth from the community as well as church members. The income was designated to underwrite the expenses of this youth ministry.

For a few, another concern emerged. Most of the "brown" bottles received came from consuming alcoholic beverages. Were we encouraging the use of alcohol by recycling this kind of glass? After discussion we felt that even if restrictions were imposed, monitoring would be impossible. So, we settled the question with more of a "shrug of the shoulder" than with any profound theological insight.

The program was a good experience for the church. In addition to the fun and fellowship, the church believes that its efforts contributed to the more extensive recycling programs of today. Our theological understanding is based on

Psalm 19:1 ". . . the earth is the Lord's . . ." and that we
are to be responsible stewards of it as mandated in Genesis
1:28, 2:15. We believed and continue to believe that recycling is a legitimate part of the mission and ministry of the
church.[6]

Equipping for Mission in the Small Church

Of course, it is the Holy Spirit who does all the equipping
for ministry. But the Holy One has been known to use human
beings in the process, and for those in a position to influence
the mission efforts of a small congregation, it might be helpful
to offer a few suggestions for coordinating with God's initia-
tives more effectively.

1. As pastors or lay leaders in a small church, it is wise to
make a clear distinction between ourselves and the Messiah.
Sometimes we fall into the trap of acting as though it is our
commitment and our efforts that are ushering in the Kingdom. What one human being can do—is called to do—for
God is limited. What one church—especially a small church—
can do is also limited. And this is as God ordained it, I sus-
pect so that, "He who boasts, let him boast in the Lord." In
the small church we need to be at peace with the fact that all
of the righteousness around us that needs doing will not be
done by us. Therefore, let us listen carefully to God's call and
not mistake the voices of compulsions or guilt or fads or our
training for God's voice. And secondly, when and if the ministry develops to the point where it can be done by the community at-large or has been successfully completed, the small
church and its leaders ought to be able to let go.

2. The pastoral role in small-church mission needs clear
definition. It is not that of "the boss," directing underlings
from a plush office. Nor is it that of the "gopher," doing for a
congregation what they say they value but are not invested in
enough to roll up their sleeves and do themselves. At different times the small-church pastor will function as a mission
catalyst, fundraiser, cheerleader, researcher, consultant, ana-
lyst, backpatter, and handholder. But I believe the small-

church pastor's primary role in relation to a congregation's mission is as co-worker. His or her position is to be alongside the folk of the congregation in their ministry efforts. The pastor can assume the mantle of companion in the effort to best advantage. When I was in seminary, the pastoral role of "enabler" was in vogue. This is a great pastoral posture because no one knows exactly what it means! What it means for the small-church pastor is to work beside his or her people in their mutual efforts to make the Kingdom more real. This co-laboring will do more to enable the congregation than the best mission-oriented sermons, guilt lavishly applied, or infinitely detailed directions. "Just do it."

3. The lifestyle of the pastor must be one of commitment, credibility, and consistency. If the pastor is perceived as not being committed to the church and its ministry context, then few in the congregation will be willing to get involved in making waves in their community only to see the pastor bail out to a bigger church. When the pastor makes a pitch for mission involvement, this pitch must be backed up with elbow grease. "What you do speaks a whole lot louder than what you say, pastor." And there needs to be a wholeness, a consistency, between one's "clergyness" and one's humanity, between one's words and one's deeds, between Sundays and weekdays.

The "person" of the pastor is an important factor in a small church's effectiveness in community ministry. Small churches can help by selecting their pastors with care not resignation, and by nurturing the personal and social "transplanting" of their pastors. Many researchers suggest that it takes from three to ten years for a new pastor to get rooted in a community.[7] Churches that can facilitate this connecting process are in a better position to effect ministry than those that impede it.

One pastor on Block Island understood his role in preparing and equipping the people of his congregation for mission, as this story of an unexpected opportunity for the ministry of hospitality reveals.

Block Island residents provided comfort to Boy Scouts who were stranded there

What began as a weekend camping trip turned into an adventure of a lifetime for some Portsmouth Boy Scouts. Thirteen Boy Scouts from Troop 1 and their four adult leaders were left stranded on Block Island the weekend of April 20-21 when a major storm system moved into the area over the weekend.

But luckily, a little island hospitality made the trip a memorable one.

On Saturday, April 20, the party took the ferry from Point Judith to a scout campsite on Block Island. After pitching their tents, the scouts toured the area by bicycle and visited several historic landmarks. But after a day's activities, the boys were greeted with a major wind and rain storm in the middle of the night. By Sunday morning the storm had intensified, and the group was told the ferry could not sail with the high tides and gale-force winds.

"They were like little drowned rats," said Linda Stimpson, the troop's publicity chairperson.

A few of the adult leaders went out looking for a safe place for the boys to stay. They were delighted when the pastor of the Old Harbor Church agreed to let them spend the night in their basement until the next day, when they could take the ferry back.

The minister and his wife offered the troop the use of their cars to go back to the campsite and collect all the tents, backpacks and other gear. While their supplies were being picked up, the boys had to peddle their bikes to the church. "The winds were so fierce, they had to peddle going downhill," said Ms. Stimpson. A local resident offered quarters to the boys so they could dry their clothes in a nearby laundromat.

Ironically, the most enjoyable part of the excursion for the boys was their stay at the church—the one part of the trip that was unplanned. The church came equipped with a television set and pool table, so understandably the boys were quite comfortable.

"They just thought it was the greatest part of the trip," said Ms. Stimpson of the church.

Finally, on Monday morning, the storm subsided and the ferry was given permission to sail. The troop is grateful to the pastor and other residents of Block Island for their assistance. "It was neat that the town jumped in to help," said Ms. Stimpson.

As for the adult leaders, they had mixed feelings about prolonging their stay. "They didn't know whether to laugh or cry or enjoy it," said Ms. Stimpson. "The kids were saying, 'Great.' The adults were saying, 'Uh-oh, we're missing work.' "[8]

Another small church, this one in Burnside, Iowa, offers their suggestions for ministry that is personal and do-able.

How One Small Church in Iowa Does Mission

Mission Note Presenter—Laypersons giving brief mission news each week at service.

Personal Witnessing—Home and hospital visits, friendly telephone calls, birthday and get-well cards, thank you notes or letters of affirmation for a job well done.

Kite Flying Festival—In the spring try this, along with a simple outdoor cookout. Include all families of the community.

Nursery Leaflets to New Parents—Quarterly leaflets from Christian Parent's Packet—"This Child of Ours" delivered by a member of the congregation each quarter.

Annual Offerings—Understanding the denominational family mission and where each local congregation fits into the broader family.

Missionary Visits—Each year host a missionary. This sharpens interest in the mission and strengthens denominational ties.

Anniversary Sunday—Honoring the business people of the community who provide the daily and weekly services; videotape of work on one of the mission fields; sharing with members of a retirement center who are guests for the day; a slide presentation of a sister church seeking support for a full-time pastor.

Friendship Haven Day—An annual event when residents of a retirement facility are transported by members of the congregation to the church for a Sunday afternoon program geared to the residents (with lots of humor) followed by refreshments and a take-home gift.

Operation: Birthday Remembrance—Remembering residents of a retirement center on their birthday with a card and gift left at their table in the dining room.

Tree Planting—On Arbor Day, a tree planting ceremony, with emphasis on good stewardship of God's creation.

Funeral Luncheons—Often become a powerful way to witness God's love to others.

Letter Exchange—With a sister church in the Area or Region. Learning of each other's work, dreams and problems. Also assuring one another of prayer support.

Lay Exchange—Lay couples exchanging visits with a sister church. Bringing greetings and sharing briefly something about the church and its work.

Adopting Seminary Student—Helps acquaint congregation with the life of a seminary student—his needs, his studies, his aspirations. His response to gifts of support—prayer and money—helps him grow in appreciation of a local church family he has never seen.[9]

Strategies for Implementation

1. Gather a group of committed church members (or speak individually with them). Ask:
   a. What are some of the ways you've helped your neighbors over the last year?
   b. What are some things you wished you could have done?
   c. What troubles you about our community?

Within the answers will be clues to the skills and behaviors of your congregation, perceived needs in the community, and the direction and level of readiness for the next ministry step.

2. Observe your congregation.

   What happens when a new person visits? when a prayer request is shared? when a need arises?

   What brings a response? What is left unattended to?

   Are there identifiable "spark plugs" for caring in the congregation? Could the "spark plugs" be helped to share their passion for caring with others?

3. The Saturday Men's Breakfast Prayer Group of a small church has decided to visit at least one person they prayed for and report back. Are there structures within your congregation that could be used to undergird personal mission?

4. Paint a word picture of the "culture" of your small church. What does it "feel" like to insiders? outsiders?

    What changes in congregational culture will encourage personal ministry?

5. Are there ways in which you can invite a personal connection between church members and the needs of others? How about: visiting a hospital, nursing home, jail or day care? attending PTA, AA, etc., meetings? chatting with people at the fire station, general store, etc.?

Chapter 4

Small-Church Mission: Pattern

Paradigms of Faithfulness

A Heavenly Interlude

"Well, God, it is happening just the way you said it would." Gabriel pulled up the cloud nearest to God and sat down.

"The whole place is falling apart. There are foreclosures and rumors of foreclosures. Farmers are going bankrupt. Suicides, nervous breakdowns, and nobody knows when it is going to end.

"Earthquakes in the financial institutions are causing tremors throughout the world. Banks have gone belly up and only insiders have got their money out. The government's bailout program needs to be bailed out itself.

"Cities, whole cities are going bankrupt, while drug use and drug profiteering are increasing. Employment is down and pollution is up.

"In the midst of millions of people, thousands are dying of loneliness. While the poor are getting poorer, the rich are getting richer and greedier.

"The government can't afford to fix any of this, so it finds one distraction after another."

God only said, "Ummm. . . ." The pain on the divine visage was too great for words.

"That's the problem. Now the plan." Gabriel was warming to his task.

"I figure history's proved beyond a shadow of a doubt that problems don't get solved from the top down—no offense, Lord. It is better to work from the bottom up. To get down to the nitty gritty, the grassroots, and build up a new consciousness, a new awareness, a new spirituality, a spirituality of caring and husbandry, of service and faithfulness, of love and work, of relationship and satisfaction with the simple joys of life. So we need to deploy into every village and hamlet, neighborhood and ghetto, a division of heaven's army, a group of God's guerrillas, a cadre of Kingdom builders, a corps of Christ's own who are touched by your Spirit and, on the other hand, who can touch their neighbors with love. . . ."

"Right, Gabriel. But I'm a step ahead of you," God said. "I've already got my army deployed in every hamlet and village, neighborhood and ghetto. Even in a couple of suburbs, too."

"You do? I haven't noticed 'em. Give me a clue, O Holy One. Who are they?" Gabriel queried.

"Why, my small churches, of course," God answered matter-of-factly. "I have strategically placed hundreds of thousands of them just for such a time as this. They need only to rise up in service to their neighbors and as leaven to society, and the Kingdom will start to happen!"

"Hmmph," grumbled Gabriel. "It's a darn good thing you believe in resurrections, Lord, because that's just what it's going to take!"

"O, Gabe, where is your faith? You said the same thing about the Twelve, remember? And that worked out. Trust me."

Strategies for "Success"

To the Jews I became as a Jew, in order to win Jews. To those under the law I became as one under the law (though I myself am not under the law) so that I might win those under the law. To those outside the law I became as one outside the law (though I am not free from God's law but am under Christ's law) so that I might win those outside the law. To the weak I became weak, that I might win the weak. I have become all things to all people, that I might by all means save some (1 Corinthians 9:20-22).

Do not be conformed to this world, but be transformed by the renewing of your minds, so that you may discern what is the will of God—what is good and acceptable and perfect (Romans 12:2).

Scripture unfortunately does not provide us an unambiguous answer to the question of accommodation. In order to share the Good *News*, Christians need to be in contact with others, speak the same language, and use at least some of the same thought forms. There has to be common ground. Christians must be *in* the world. But in order to have *Good* News to share, Christians and their social structures must be different from the society to which they are speaking. We must have something godly to offer to the faithlessness of this generation; we must have something healthy to confront dysfunctional patterns; we must have something fresh to "wake up" an inert society; we must have something righteous to proclaim in the midst of social inequality. Christians must not be *of* the world, but we must be in it.

Large churches are in a position to speak to larger numbers of people in the world. Yet inherent in the scale of their operations is the need to adapt to the language, mores, and infrastructure of the culture. For that very fact they may actually have less to say, since the greater the degree of adaptation to the dominant society, the less leaven is left in the message. And because the medium is the message (a truth we Christians discerned in the Incarnation of Jesus well before Marshall McLuhan expressed it), the message of the large church is conditioned by its organizational and cultural reality.

The story is told of two horse ranchers who were bitter rivals. They had arranged for a head-to-head race, and each owner was going all out. One had hired a renowned professional jockey. Each had bet his ranch on his horse. From the starting gun the horses raced neck and neck. On the far turn, though, they bumped. Both horses fell, throwing their jockeys. The professional jockey jumped back into the saddle and galloped for the finish line. He crossed it while the other jockey still sat in the dust. The winning jockey's jubilation turned to confusion, however, when he saw the rage and disgust on the face of the owner who'd hired him. "What's wrong, boss? I won, didn't I?"

"You fool!" cried the boss. "You won, but I didn't. You jumped on the wrong horse!"

Just so, if we are riding the wrong horse, the more successful we are, the less successful we are. Some of our more "successful" churches may have become so by riding society's horse, not God's. For example, consider three current strategies of "successful" churches.

1. *Success breeds success.*

Our dominant culture loves winners and assigns agony to defeat. Nobody wants to be a loser. Failure *is* fatal in our society. Unemployed people are not just unemployed; they feel unworthy and are treated as undeserving. According to *Newsweek*, even in their choice of churches people want to identify with success:

> Church Growth Movement experts judge a minister's accountability not by his faithfulness to the Gospel but whether, as Schaller puts it, "the people keep coming and giving." By that measure, the most successful churches are those that most resemble a suburban mall. What works best, according to the CGM, is a one-stop church complex that offers an array of affinity groups where individuals can satisfy their need for intimacy yet identify with a large, successful enterprise. The ideal advocated by the CGM is the megachurch, a total environment under a single, sacred canopy.[1]

Some attendees of these one-stop churches may wonder about the vestigial artistry depicting a young man executed for failing to negotiate the political and religious system of his day. Must be a graphic reminder of the price of failure!

2. *Like attracts like.*

Many larger churches have grown and continue to grow on the basis of the "homogeneity principle." This principle states that people are attracted to join groups that are composed of people like themselves. This principle is true—in that it describes reality. People's anxieties or fears are aroused, or needs fail to be met, when they are confronted with others who are perceived to be different from themselves. So organizations will grow if they concentrate their energies in recruiting people like themselves and avoid wasting energy in trying to build bridges or break down barriers with people who are different. (Of course, when Paul wrote "There is no longer Jew or Greek, there is no longer slave or free, there is no longer male and female; for all of you are one in Christ Jesus" (Galatians 3:28), he must have been referring to heaven. Such idealism is impractical on earth.)

3. *When in Rome.*

Baby boomers have taken over the world, and this phenomenon is prolifically, if not adequately, covered in church literature. Churches are counseled to meet the boomers on their own turf. For example, boomers are not known for long-term commitments. So an invitation to a weekly Sunday school class is unlikely to be accepted, but a one to four-week study might be. Boomers worship relevancy. So "Overcoming Dysfunctional Relationships" will sell a lot better than "Diamonds from Deuteronomy." And boomers must see the benefit. "Duty" and "right" won't motivate, but "gain" and "payoff" might. Thus, although boomers are by definition already "O.K.," an appeal to improved relationships in a four-week study group might sell.

A strategy of church programming that includes immediacy, low commitment, and high self-benefit might connect with boomers, but a church that offers no alterative to their present way of life will not be redemptive to them. A friend of mine pastors a middle-sized church in an affluent suburb of a large New England city. He was a businessman before he felt the call to pastoral ministry. He pastors the "prestigious" church in his town, filled with high-level business executives. He knows how to speak their language. In fact, he knows how to incarnate their structures and methods of operating. With great excitement he shared with me the reorganization plan for his church. Boards were being replaced with departments (Department of Buildings and Grounds, Department of Human Resources, Department of Outreach Ministries). The bylaws section on church officers was being replaced by job descriptions and portfolios. And on and on. When accomplished, the reorganization will have increased efficiency (a dominant cultural value) and the church will be comprehensible to the business world. Indeed, that church will have been remade in its likeness.

And what's wrong with that? Well, only four things! The dominant society is indulgent, impersonal, disembodied, and disconnected. Of course, other than that, it's not too bad! But if the church is all too often being remade in the image of the world, what are some of the elements that would need to become cultural realities for the Kingdom of God to be embodied in our society?

One element is the idea of limits. Our nation has come to its geographical limits. We have run out of frontiers. Our supplies of crude oil, uranium, and other elements are large but finite. There are limits to the amount of pollution that nature can absorb, and there are limits to how many people will starve before those who have too little will rise up against those who have too much. If a viable and righteous order is to come out of the present age, it will be an order that knows how to live with limits: material, psychological, and social.

Another element can be summarized in the expression "human scale." We live in a day and age when computer numbers are more important than our names, when people can die in their apartments and not be discovered for weeks, where the means of production are so vast that workers are merely cogs on a wheel. Some have called us a nation of strangers, but no nation that is foreign to the human needs of its citizens will long survive. People need to be bound to one another in personal, human ways. If a sustainable order is to come out of the present age, it must find a way to allow each of us to be a person, to have a place, and to be a part of a caring family.

A third element emphasizes the grassroots over the bureaucratic. Local people know their needs and their resources. The results of handing our responsibility over to Washington, Wall Street, Madison Avenue, or even town hall are all too obvious. If the Kingdom is to emerge out of the present age, local groups must organize themselves and take responsibility for the shape of their future.

A fourth element has to do with connections. The trend of our society over the past few decades has been to break down ties of the family and community and replace them with impersonal, ineffectual, one-way connections. I pay taxes to Washington, but what control do I have? I watch TV, but what impact do I as a viewer really have? I may refuse to buy Brand X, but if Brand Y is the same product, what real options are left to me? We need to develop connections that are capable of two-way communication, that are mutually responsible, and that are interdependent.

Former U.S. Senator Paul Tsongas, in his book *The Road From Here*, says that our society is like a boat blissfully steaming down river, unaware that just ahead of us is a waterfall that will dash our ship to pieces.[2] If we are to avoid this fate, then our society needs to be reordered. We need a social structure that knows how to live within its limits, one that is personal, indigenous, and interdependent. In short, society needs to be organized on biblical principles.

The Redeeming Elements of Small-Church Life

The values of our dominant culture set the pace for society. But the small church marches to the beat of a different drummer. The small church, then, tends not to be registered by dominant culture-shaped structures, or if registered, then not heard, and if heard, not valued. Yet the small church has a significant message to convey for this very reason. While it has only whispered into the cacophony of society, it whispers words of salvation. Its medium is redemptive. Its life is leaven. "In a big world, the small church has remained *intimate*. In a fast world, the small church has been *steady*. In an expensive world, the small church has remained *plain*. In a rational world, the small church has kept *feeling*. In a mobile world, the small church has been an *anchor*. In an anonymous world, the small church *calls us by name*."[3]

Small-church life incarnates a particular way of living in the world and that way, because it is so refreshingly, radically different from our dominant culture, is God's leaven. I believe God is calling the small church to permeate and transform our culture by offering it a pattern for righteous living. This pattern, found in the social structure of the small church, embodies four redeeming qualities: living within limits, living in personal relationship, living in indigenous social structures, and living with interdependent social relations.

Living Within Limits

The small church is used to living with limits: it is by its very nature limited, and everyone, friend and enemy alike, knows the limits of the small church. Limited budget, limited personnel, limited options. But we kick against the limits— cursing our fuel bills, and devising elaborate schemes to lump parishes together. What if we learned to live *within* our limits? What if one organization in American society lived joyfully and creatively and constructively in its finiteness? What a power for transformation and redemption that would be! The small church is by its very nature limited, and we can praise God for it, as this church in Maine learned to do.

An Example of Living Creatively at the Margins: A Pile of Slippers

They were factory rejects, but gratefully accepted by the West Bowdoin congregation. Instead of ending their days at a landfill, one thousand slippers were dumped at the church's community building; they were rescued and redeemed.

The next day a dozen members of the congregation started sorting over the slippers by size and color. In a few days three hundred pairs had been matched up. Two days earlier the women's mission circle had decided to include the native Maine children of the Aroostook Band of Mic-Macs on their Christmas list. With only $50 in the postage fund, how could thirteen cartons be sent to Presque Isle?

One member, an officer in the Maine National Guard, offered the services of the Guard; another suggested that her employer, UPS, might want to help. By December 18th the slippers, along with others gifts of mittens, caps, and toys, were heading for The County.

Enough slippers were left over for a box full for the Bowdoin Town Welfare, a supply for the elementary school for use on cold, wet days, and several cartons for the Lisbon area interchurch clothing bank.

God is still in the renewal business. Not only does God find a new home and usefulness for slipper rejects, but God has a promise and a plan for a new life and a second chance for every person.[4]

Living in Personal Relationship

The small church is by its very nature personal. In a day and age when people are no more than machines to their employers, numbers to their government, and pledges to their church, what a blessing it is to find one organization that is fully and unashamedly personal, even if quaint, old fashioned, and not always loving. Simply by living out who we are as a small church—a group of people who know and care about each other—we will shine as a light in the land of darkness, we will well up like living waters in a parched and dry land. The small church is by its very nature personal, and we can thank God for it.

One small church in Michigan, the Benton Harbor Presbyterian Church, learned that they could indeed be a light in the darkness by starting where they were and changing what they could through personal ministry. They developed the following "Personal Principles of Outreach Ministry":

Look at the Big Picture, Start with the Small Program

After assessing the wide spectrum of needs facing those who live around you, start with a small program focused on real people with their definable needs.

Keep It Personal

Outreach ministry should never move beyond the point where the personal touch of contact and caring gets lost in providing the service.

Let the Personal Lead to Public Policy

As you become involved in the personal lives of those you serve, you will become aware of the public policy issues that often lie behind their situation. Helping to change society is as important as the personal touch.

I Take a Step in Your Direction, You Take a Step in Mine

As you care for others, allow or provide them ways to care for themselves. Your "step in their direction" is your unconditional care for them. Their "step in your direction" is their learning to care for their own life—and perhaps for you!

Not on the Basis of Deserving, but of Need

Who are we to judge who "deserves" our care and who doesn't? All God's children deserve our care. So offer care in response to needs, without judgment, though there may be times when you are able to determine whether or not someone "needs" a particular kind of care. Sometimes, not to help someone is to help them.

Three Strikes and You're Out

You'll be taken advantage of from time to time. Expect it. Its part of the game. But don't let it go on forever. Play it like baseball. Three strikes and you're out.

Live the Gospel through Outreach, Share the Gospel through Worship

The purpose of outreach is to share the good news of God's gracious love through actions, not preaching. Invite those you care for to worship, where they can then hear about the good news they've already experienced through your care. If they won't come to church, they probably aren't ready to hear about the gospel anyway.

Not Only for Their Sake, But for Your Sake As Well

When one of God's children is hurting, all of God's children are less than what God intended. So when you reach out to someone, you are not only doing it for their sake, but for yours as well.

Let God Change Others, Let Outreach Ministry Change You

Outreach ministry should not be one way. You hope that people's lives will be changed by your care, but for the relationship to be genuine, the process must be mutually transformative. Let God take care of changing the people you serve. Work on changing yourself—your attitudes, perspectives, values, priorities—through the experience of serving others.

Inner Journey, Outer Journey

As you engage in the "outer journey" of service and outreach, you must engage in the "inner journey" of prayer, reflection, and personal transformation. And now, instead of praying because "you're supposed to," being engaged in the lives of others gives you someone to pray for.

"Better to Light a Candle Than Curse the Darkness"

This is the motto of the American Friends Society. It is one, at least hopeful way to confront the darkness of our world. And it really strikes at the heart of Christian faith. As one of the gospels puts it: "The light shines in the darkness, and the darkness has not overcome it." It doesn't say the light does away with the darkness. It shines in it. And is not overcome.[5]

Living in Indigenous Social Structures

The small church is by its very nature indigenous. I know the small church can be insular and anachronistic. It can be peculiar and idiosyncratic, and oftentimes it's stubborn and sinful. Yet it is the one group in every town or neighborhood that is absolutely local. It is the one group that reflects the character of the community. It is the one organization that you can count on to be grassroots in nature, much to the frustration of many a denominational executive! The indigenous nature of the small church can be used to stifle obedience, but it can also be used to incarnate the love of God in *the form appropriate to its setting.* The small church, by its very nature, is indigenous and we can thank God for it.

The Rev. Christina Del Piero, pastor of St. Paul's United Church of Christ, a small inner-city congregation in the East Bronx, had this story to tell about the power of indigenous mission in the small church:

Grassroots: Responding to Local Needs

Recently one of my parishioners told me with a proud smile that I am becoming known as the "garbage pastor," and maybe, by implication, that St. Paul's is becoming known as the garbage church!

We have garbage all around us in a part of the city strewn with evidence that humanity is trashing the Earth—abandoned buildings, junked cars, streets littered with fast-food wrappers and soda cans. We share a panorama of garbage to which we cannot shut our eyes, and we also share a love for the Earth.

The story itself begins several months before the United Nations Environmental Sabbath, celebrated in June 1989, when I participated in a gathering of people connected to inner-city communities who had been asked how the Environmental Sabbath might reach urban people. I was inspired by the challenge and by the discussion, so, using some of the UNES materials and a bit of courageous imagination, I decided to create a liturgy that included the invitation to the congregation to bring a gift of creation to the church for the Environmental Sabbath.

The response was overwhelming—children brought apples, stones, and flowers; a woman in her late eighties brought three little bowls, one with lentils, one with rice, and one with barley; a man brought a shell with a note in it that his grandfather had carried it from China during the Boxer Rebellion in the late 1800s. There were fossils and ears of corn, a maple tree one woman had potted from her son's house in the country, squash, quartz crystals, sand, and an orange.

When the time for my sermon came, I stood by the altar naming some of the gifts and telling their stories. Then I began to quote statistics about the disposable diapers, plastic pens, aluminum cans, and Styrofoam that we dump on the Earth. I took a bag of garbage—Clorox bottles, junk mail, plastic dinner utensils, frozen dinner boxes, soup cans—and with a clatter and a bang, dumped it around the altar which held the gifts of creation.

People gasped (even my own knees shook a bit!) and I said to the congregation, "You gasp because I have desecrated our altar, and our altar is a symbol of what is holy. Every day we desecrate the Earth, which is not a symbol of the holy; the Earth is holy; the Earth is God's own creation. The Earth suffocates under this garbage; she cries acid tears." I then showed them a photograph of the Earth from space and read what an astronaut has written about how alive and fragile it looks. I showed them a painting of the Earth crying and played a part of the Faure *Requiem* which sounds to me like the Earth crying out. We sat looking at the garbage around our sanctuary, a place we work hard to keep neat and clean, a place of order in a broken and chaotic city.

I then lit a candle and talked about the fact that we do care, that our caring is the beginning of our hope that we can save the Earth and let her rest. I blessed bread with the words of a wheat farmer in Kansas: "This bread comes from wheat which comes from the Earth. Our bodies will return to the Earth. Between the time when we eat this bread from the Earth and our bodies return to the Earth, we can save the Earth." The children then distributed the bread, asking people to say, "We will save the Earth" as they passed the bread to each other. . . .

I cannot say that we are doing a lot, but we are seeing ourselves in a new light, maybe re-rooting ourselves in order to bear fruit of a new kind. The two key ministries of the church are now interpreted in environmental terms; we tend a large garden for the East Bronx Hunger Program, growing tomatoes, potatoes, carrots, beans, and peppers for hungry people in our area; the Women's Guild runs about six rummage sales a year which not only provide most of my base salary, but which also provide a neighborhood recycling process.[6]

Living with Interdependent Social Relations

Lastly, the small church, if it is to fulfill its nature, must be interdependent. But here we have failed our calling. Instead of rejoicing in each other's strengths, sharing and working together, and staying in communication, we have allowed ourselves to become separated. We have severed ourselves from each other. Often we cower, each in our own corner, jealous, competitive, insecure, and defensive. We have accepted the world's criteria of success as numerical bigness and independence, when we should have aimed for God's criteria of faithfulness and mutual interdependence. As small churches we are not called to offer something for everyone. We are called to be our unique selves and join with other churches so that *together* we might be all God has in mind.

Consider this report from six Iowa churches who have something to say about working interdependently:

Interconnected

This fall Prairie Fire launched another major new program in cooperation with six Iowa church denominations. *Renewing Rural Iowa*, under development for two years, has as its goal the revitalization of rural communities through active participation of rural congregations in community issues and concerns that they themselves identify. Now underway in economically hard-hit southern Iowa, this ecumenical project has the eye and support of state and national church agencies committed to finding new ways to rebuild rural communities and congregations.

The year 1991 also saw the *Church Land Project* move into full swing. This unique, joint project of Prairie Fire and the National Catholic Rural Life Conference, is committed to development of new ways to help religious institutions care for the land they own. The project is helping churches develop new policies and programs for their land, based on stewardship and conservation practices and a commitment to family farm agriculture. The grassroots, hands on approach of the project means that the members of participating churches are implementing the process on their own terms, specific to their own situation and needs.[7]

Agent of Transformation

The transforming power of God can be seen at work in so many small churches. On Block Island, for example, we are a lopsided resort community. We suffer greatly under economic inequities between the wealthy vacationers and the poor year-rounders. But the Harbor Church, through its members, its boards, and its buildings, is struggling equally to redress the imbalances. We have helped form a food cooperative, an arts and crafts guild, and a nonprofit employment organization. We are working on equitable housing, and we are laying the groundwork for a mechanism to shape our own future.

In Burnside, Iowa, the twelve or so families that comprise the Baptist church there have found an entirely different way to minister to their community. Annually, they pick a biblical theme that illumines their daily life. Then they go to town with it. Literally. A few years ago, their theme was "Thankful Living." They invited the whole town to celebrate an "Appreciation Day." In a public ceremony, individuals, organizations, and businesses were thanked for their efforts toward the common good. Two years later, a reporter remarked that in a community that had begun to give up on itself, that single, simple ceremony instilled hope for the future in the whole town.

In a small town in the Berkshire mountains, trouble was brewing. A group of "hippies" (to use a sixties' term) had moved in to that staid New England community, and the stage was set for polarization, hostility, and hatred. But the part-time pastor of the little church in town went and visited these flower children and got to know them. Then he organized a monthly "Alterative Lifestyle" supper. At first, only the hippies bothered to attend, but gradually church members began to drop in and then some community folk. There they shared their mutual concerns, and personal and philosophical bridges began to be built. Reconciliation happened not only between groups, but between value systems. The old New Englanders became more concerned about issues like alternative energy, and the flower children grew into responsible parents and citizens. So effective was that little church in motivating the whole community to a lifestyle of stewardship that the governor asked the town to represent the state in an energy conservation contest.

And the list goes on and on: small churches starting firewood cooperatives in New Hampshire; forming credit unions in inner-city Philadelphia; reaching out to heal the hurts of the community in Hastings, Iowa. These small churches have made a difference in the world in which they live.

I believe that the church's mission is to participate with God in the transformation of human life, both corporate and individual. And I believe that the small church, by its very nature as a grassroots, personal, interconnected, and limited form, can be the leaven of transformation if we are faithful.

But not all small churches. Some will die, because they have put their facilities above faithfulness, their survival above service, their past above God's future. Some will lose their buildings and become house churches. Some will have to change their museum mentality and open their doors to their needy neighbors. Some must give up their wish to have a pastor-messiah lead them into the promised land of bigness. Some need to reach back into a rich heritage and learn anew what it means to be lay-led.

We can neutralize this great calling to be agents of transformation by our feeling of impotence. We really don't believe that we can effect God's will: we are so small and limited and composed of such "characters." Our self-analysis repeats the conclusion of a denominational official: we are without the "financial, material and human resources to engage in a meaningful program."[8] Especially, we might add, a mission program.

We are like the servant of Elisha, who on waking early one morning saw that his city was surrounded by the army of the enemy. All in a dither, he ran to Elisha and blurted, "My Lord, what are we to do?" Elisha chuckled and told the servant to calm his fears. Then he prayed that God would open his eyes that he might see things as they truly were, not as limited human vision reduced them. The Lord answered Elisha's prayer, and the eyes of the servant were opened and he saw things from God's perspective, and there surrounding him on all sides, ranging on the mountains as far as the eye could see, were "horses and chariots of fire" (2 Kings 6:17). The army of the Lord, invisible except to the eyes of faith, was there insuring the victory for God's faithful people.

The small church will have to die to itself if it is to live again as God's agent of transformation. But I believe that this can be our destiny. In the first century God used a vast network of small churches to "turn the whole world upside down." In the middle of this century God used a vast array of house churches to transform the nation of China. And I believe that this is God's pattern and plan for us, too.

We might wonder about our tomorrow. We might despair for the future of our church, we might have lost hope for our community, but God has ranged throughout our nation an army, invisible to the eyes of this world, but mighty and powerful, to effect his will. And brothers and sisters of the small church, we are that army!

Strategies for Implementation

1. God's people, especially those in small churches, are called to live out of an alternative reality to the dominant culture. In the communication methods of your congregation (preaching, teaching, newsletter, etc.), what is being done to articulate and affirm Kingdom values and behaviors?

2. In what ways could your congregation turn its liabilities (by worldly standards) into assets (by biblical standards)? For example, a congregation with a self-demeaning "second fiddle" mentality might come to see itself positively as a family church.

3. What celebrations of alternatives could your church have, like the Appreciation Day the Burnside Baptist Church hosted for their community?

4. Could your congregation provide an impetus for alterna-

tive ways of living: literature, workshops, retreats, celebrations, fairs, forums, etc.?

5. Review the behavior of your congregation. In what ways
do you live out of your limitations, personhood, grassroots
nature, and interdependence? In what ways could you be
more harmonious with those values?

Chapter 5

Small Church Mission: Program

Organizing for Community Impact

People launch community ministries because they care—not just rationally, but with powerful compassion.

—Carl S. Dudley,
in *Basic Steps Toward Community Ministry*[1]

Two Churches Doing Community Ministry

Small churches in this country are doing good work in community ministries such as organizing food banks and joining in neighborhood coalitions to fight drug abuse. Size is not the most significant factor in these ministries: a community ministry can be an elderly telephone chain which costs little, or a highly organized, church-based social service agency funded by multiple sources. What is required are a few people with vision and what Carl Dudley describes as "powerful compassion."

In this chapter we describe the steps that are important for organizing community ministries, which we define as organized programs and activities that address needs in the community outside of the congregation. These ministries might originate from concerns expressed within the congregation— a member laid off the job as the result of a factory closing, for example—but in their life they embrace the larger community.

What is unique about the role of a small church's participation in community ministry is that it can't do it alone. By its nature of limited resources and few people, small churches must form partnerships with other churches and organizations. At the heart of small-church community ministry is cooperation.

We begin our exploration of the small church's involvement in community ministries with two examples, one rural, one urban.

"To Reach the Last House on the Last Road . . ."

Carl Geores, pastor of the Leeds Community Church in central Maine, knew exactly what he was doing when he asked elder Charles Woodward to pick up five children and drive them to Sunday school. The children lived at the end of a dirt road in an abandoned cabin. On a cold December Sunday morning Charles found the family huddled around a smoky wood stove; the inside temperature was only a few degrees higher than the frigid outside. The elder was shocked by what he saw: a family living in a cold, dirt-floor shack. After the worship service that Sunday, he reported back to the minister, "We have to do something to help that family." A week later, men from the church spent two days insulating the house. Later they replaced the wood stove and dug a well, and deacons helped out with food and new clothing.

"I didn't know people lived like that in our town," the elder told the church governing board. Thus, from one layperson's shocked sensitivities, a housing ministry was born. Men from this small, rural church began to spend weekends working on neighbors' substandard homes. Materials were donated by local lumberyards; deacons raised money.

In time the housing ministry grew to encompass eight communities, and the range of services expanded to include a thrift shop. Today, twenty years later, an elder's dream has developed into the Rural Community Action Ministry, a nonprofit social service agency that provides services to twelve rural communities.

"Helping a Church Find a New Life"

Grace Presbyterian Church is a lovely gothic, stone church located on a tree-lined boulevard in downtown Kansas City, Missouri. The band leading the congregation in a lively hymn seems out of place in the dark-paneled, solemn sanctuary. The spirited multiracial congregation enjoying the morning worship service is very different from the church founders, their names now etched into the stained-glass windows. Indeed, Grace Church nearly died. Like many other urban congregations, when the neighborhood began to change, the white congregation fled the city for the suburbs.

But Grace Church did not die. Instead, it began to minister to the needs of its changing community. Today Grace Church, a merger of two congregations, Methodist and Presbyterian, has a membership of one hundred twenty. It sponsors the largest food pantry in Kansas City, serving meals to fifteen hundred people each month.

Pastor Sharon Garfield loves the excitement that fills every corner of Grace Church. "We're focusing on the needs of children," she told me after morning worship. "Last summer we started a vacation Bible school. I went out into the community and invited children. After an hour I had over one hundred sign up; *they all came*. In the fall we organized a Sunday school and we have seventy-five children coming each week. Twice a week, the church hosts an afternoon program for children. We focus on building self-esteem and raising awareness of their cultural and racial gifts. There is a lot of tension in this community. The children live with violence and abuse. We want them to come to this church and know something different.

"The woman who leads the Sunday school writes all the curriculum. The teachers meet Saturday afternoon, review the material, then they meet for prayer and support.

"What is so hopeful about Grace Church is that the people who run our programs have become members. All of the teachers in the Sunday school have joined the church. That's where our membership comes from now, from the community right around Grace Church."

When asked what revitalized Grace Church, Pastor Garfield is quick to give much of the credit to her predecessor.

"He understood that Grace Church, an affluent white congregation, was dying, and he led the dwindling congregation through a death process. He helped them remember and celebrate their heritage, but he told them they could never be that again. He gave them a vision of something new, a church that ministered to a changing community. When I was called to this church, the congregation was very welcoming to me, and accepting of the new people in the community."

Sharon was trained and worked as a community organizer before being ordained by the Methodist Church. She puts her organizational skills to good advantage. "My style is to help people find their ministries. I prefer to be in the background, not in the spotlight. I love to hang out at the food closet, or drop in at community meeting places. I listen and find out what people need, and then go to work. Some programs, like the weekday youth center, Grace can do alone; other things like a shelter for battered women or the soup kitchen at the Lutheran church, we work together on. I believe the church needs to live out in this community what it professes on Sunday morning."[3]

Your Community Ministry

These examples of two small churches actively engaged in community ministries show that small churches have an important role to play in their communities. Our experience has been that when congregations become involved in such ministries, they move beyond survival.

When you ask the people who attend the Leeds and Grace churches to describe their congregations' ministries, they almost burst with excitement. They speak with pride about the compassion that is shown to the poor. The people of these two churches can tell you in detail what they are doing in the community. When pressed, they will acknowledge that the church could use a few new members, that the roof leaks and the budget is tight. But those concerns do not define their understanding of their church. The first word spoken is the importance the congregation places on ministry to the community. A lay leader in the Leeds church summed up her satisfaction with her small congregation, "People in the community are amazed at what the church is doing."

Based on the experiences of the Leeds and Grace churches, we propose a six-step process to help your church identify and organize its unique community ministry. First we will summarize each step in the process, then explore each step in greater detail.

1. Understand Your Community's Needs

The first step to identifying your congregation's community ministry is to learn about the surrounding community's needs. Every block, neighborhood, village, and town is distinct. Begin by identifying the particular needs of your community. In rural Leeds, Maine, a community needed decent housing. In the neighborhood around Grace Church, a community need cried out on every street corner where children hung out with nothing to do after school. Such community needs can be learned by simply driving around town and making a "windshield survey." Make a list of needs you see right around you. Add to it an assessment of what has changed in the neighborhood over the last ten years. What businesses are opening or closing? Who is moving in or out of town? Ask yourself what is likely to happen in the next ten years. This list of needs and trends we call your *possibilities for ministry.*

2. Understand Your Congregation's Story

The second step is to identify what is unique about your congregation. Begin by remembering your church's story. Under what circumstances was your congregation founded? What have been the "defining moments" in its history? Next describe your church as it is today. Who comes to church? Where do they live? How much money is available for new ministries? Is the church building suitable for programs? The organizing credo for the Leeds church was "to reach the last house on the last road." The congregation was proud of its legacy of hospitality to strangers. When the church embarked on a housing ministry, they saw this ministry as a continuation of its covenant. Your congregation's story, past and present, we call your *potential for ministry*.

3. Define the Need Your Congregation Can Meet

The third step is the creative part of the process. After you have listed community needs, described your congregation's story, and listed your resources, you match the *possibilities* for ministry with your church's *potential*. Grace Church had a long history of summer vacation Bible schools. That was the church's *potential*. A clear community need or *possibility* for ministry was the presence of children hanging out on street corners. The match was coming up with the idea of a summer vacation Bible school for neighborhood children.

The three steps outlined so far help you identify your community ministry. The next three steps help you put together a plan to get started.

4. Identify the Leadership to Make Your Ministry Go

In the process we are describing, considerable care is taken to identify community ministries that your church understands as its *calling to ministry*. A key to getting started is identifying leaders who feel called to this ministry. In both the Leeds and Grace examples, one or two leaders were identified, trained, and supported to carry out their ministry.

5. Develop a Vision to Inspire

By identifying the community ministry as the church's *calling*, we are being explicitly theological. Jesus was called to his ministry through baptism and commissioning. Building a theological foundation for community ministry roots the ministry in the congregation's professed theological identity. The purpose of this step is to justify the proposed ministry as central to the mission of the church. The leadership, clergy and lay, of both the Leeds and Grace churches can articulate a clear biblical and theological understanding of why their congregations support community ministries.

6. Build Cooperation That Leads to Lasting Results

The sixth step in our process is developing adequate resources of money, materials, and staff to carry out successful community ministries. Sometimes small churches can go it alone in developing community ministries. It is our experience, however, and certainly that of the Leeds and Grace churches, that lasting ministries require building partnerships or coalitions. Partnerships can occur among churches, as in cooperative parishes, or with social service institutions. Sometimes new institutions need to be created, or new partners added to existing ones. Getting started in a community-based ministry is well within a small congregation's reach. Often the small church, because of its grassroots ties to the community, is better able than other local institutions to identify a need. Because the members see the local situation firsthand, an appropriate role for the small church in community ministry is serving as an advocate for people who are hurting, not letting the larger community forget its responsibility. But some situations may require direct action.

Steps to Getting Started in Community Ministry

We will now discuss these six steps in detail, describing an in-depth process by which your congregation can begin to find and define its own community ministry. The six steps do not represent a strict order to be followed; however, work in each area is essential to establishing a successful ministry. The steps are suggestions to help your congregation get started in community ministry.

For example, a cluster of churches in upper New York state that used this approach initially invested considerable time in studying biblical texts that focused attention on the local congregation in mission. Only after laying this biblical/theological groundwork did the group begin to look at needs within their region. This cluster of churches found that the work required patience, but the results were significant. There was renewed enthusiasm among the churches for ministry, and solid accomplishments followed.

Step 1: Understand Your Community's Needs

The kind of mission we will be describing in this chapter is "community ministry." By community ministry we mean programs that address needs in the community outside the congregation, and that are organized and carried on by a church acting alone or as part of a coalition with other churches or social agencies.

Sometimes it is difficult to see mission within our own community. Mission is something done elsewhere, in another part of the world. We think of mission as giving money to support a church in Kenya or taking up an offering for famine relief in the Sudan. Maybe it is easier to do mission far away because it simply involves raising money or making bandages or packing up food boxes. We can imagine the people who will receive our aid, but we never meet them face-to-face. Doing mission at home, in your own town, can be more difficult because you meet the people you are trying to help.

Let us start with an example. A local factory closes down operations and people from your church lose jobs. You hear that several families are having financial difficulties. The church responds by taking meals into these families' homes. The need for food grows, and at a vestry meeting someone proposes opening a food closet in the church basement.

You appeal for food during Sunday worship, shelves are built, a committee is formed to set up guidelines, volunteers are organized to staff the food closet, and you open.

People who usually don't come into your church now come and ask for a box of food. They are not like you. You meet single parents who arrive with small children. You meet people who have been released from mental institutions and have no place to live. Some people are polite and say thank you; others are pushy and demand more than you can give.

As you box up food you listen to a neighbor's story about how the grocery store check-out man is rude when she pays with food stamps. You learn what living on a fixed income is like. You hear about being evicted from an apartment for want of a security deposit, about waiting for hours with a sick child in the hospital emergency room because he does not have his own doctor. You learn a new language: AFDC, Medicaid, child protective worker. Before long the food closet committee is asking for donations of clothing to help a family who has no winter coats, and after that you are organizing a transportation network to drive single parents to the clinic or to meet the food stamp worker. A world opens up for your church that you did not know existed.

Your church sees the need to expand the hours of the food closet from one morning a week to every day. Another group in the church offers to organize a thrift shop in a storefront downtown; volunteers from the food closet begin to advocate at the town council for higher welfare payments. Soon your church is known around town as "the church that helps poor people." Social workers start calling for help: Is there someone who could take an abused child for a few days? A few families who bought clothing at the thrift shop show up for church.

What is exciting about local mission is that one opportunity leads to another. People in the church see what is happening and they get excited. The survival mentality—"how are we going to pay the bills this month?"—is replaced by a renewed sense of worth, of mission. Even more important, the community sees what is happening. That small church becomes the church that helps people, and people start to come.

Is this illustration a dream? No. We know the church where this revitalization happened, and it occurred because someone saw members of the congregation who were hurting and hungry and took them supper. The joy of local mission is that you never know where it will lead.

The first step in establishing a community ministry is seeing the need. We learn about needs by careful community analysis; sometimes the needs overtake us.

• **Respond to Crisis**

Probably the most common way a church gets started in community ministry is by responding to a crisis. A crisis can be a real opportunity for a church. It can be the event that shapes a church's direction and identity for decades to come. Churches that for years have had unnoticed, faithful ministries of presence can suddenly spring into action. Something happens in the congregation or the community that forces the church to act. A factory closes and overnight half the church membership is unemployed, and the church responds by opening a food closet or offering space for an unemployment office. A flood sweeps through a valley and destroys a trailer park, and the church is needed to house suddenly homeless families. An older couple becomes ill, and volunteers are needed to drive them to the hospital.

Earlier we mentioned a powerful example of a congregation's response to a crisis in the work of the Protestant church in LeChambon, France, described in the book *Lest Innocent Blood Be Shed* by Philip Hallie.[4] This small Huguenot church in the south of France developed an underground network that hid and saved literally thousands of Jewish children during World War II. The church's heroic action stemmed from years of simply being a faithful church.

In one rural town, our small church had an ongoing outreach ministry for years along the one muddy street of the low-income neighborhood referred to as the "ghetto." We did simple things for the residents—drove children to vacation Bible school, helped families with home heating oil, brought layettes to a family with a newborn. So when an elder learned that the ghetto had been condemned and forty poor families without any other place to live would be displaced if the area were to be demolished, it was natural for her to take the concern to the congregation. Her compassion led to the formation of a coalition of churches and social service agencies. (How this coalition developed will be shared below under step 6.) It bought the neighborhood, revitalized it, and today manages the community for low-income families. Without the crisis we would have debated the merits of our involvement in an affordable housing ministry for years and little would have happened.

Why do some churches respond to a crisis and turn it into an opportunity for ministry, while others do not see the need?

Many factors influence a congregation's readiness to risk

beginning a community ministry. The Huguenot church of LeChambon had a long history of experiencing religious oppression, which helped them recognize the desperate plight of the Jewish refugees. But historical memory is not enough. It must be given shape and substance in contemporary experience. The pastoral leadership of Andre Trocme prepared the LeChambon congregation for their courageous ministry. Through years of preaching and teaching, and by personal example, Pastor Trocme prepared the groundwork for what one parishioner described as "nothing special" in providing refuge for Jews.

In every case we know of a congregation becoming involved in community ministry, there had been careful preparation. When the opportunity came along, the church recognized their ministry. This preparation can build upon the congregation's historical memory, but it is always nurtured by preaching, teaching, and examples set forth by church leaders. When the opportunity to begin ministry arrives, it is recognizable.

• **Take a Walk Around Town**

But what if you don't have a crisis? If there is no immediate need or crisis calling your congregation into action, then it is important to search out the *possibilities for ministry* in your community. Detailed mission studies are very helpful, but they take time. We suggest a more informal approach. Ask a few people to go out with you to look around town and see what's going on.

Every summer our three-church parish employs a seminary intern. As part of the interview, seminarians are driven around the community where they will be working, and asked, "What did you see?" and "What are your impressions of the community?" The interviewing committee can usually tell immediately which student to hire. Most will make general comments, but a few will comment on the isolation of the community and poor housing. They will ask questions about where people work, how far children are bused to school, what social services are available to the town.

Seminary students are trained to understand the nature of the church, but rarely are they equipped with skills to understand the culture of a particular church's community. One of the goals of our seminary internship is to train students to understand the nature of the community. In much the same way, churches need to be trained to look around their community.

A simple way to begin is to take a "windshield survey." Drive around the neighborhood or walk around the block. What do you see? What are the physical boundaries of your community? What are the major institutions? Who lives in the block? Where do people work and where do they gather?

The next step in understanding your community is to listen to people. Ask questions; conduct an informal survey.

Douglas A. Walrath suggests preparing a worksheet. Think about the neighborhood around your church building, especially *changes in population*—growth or decline in numbers, and changes in ethnic groups; *buildings* that have gone up or have deteriorated or were torn down; *institutions* in the area—what they are and are not doing, and how they are changing (include other churches); and *transportation*—changes in the roads or types of transportation available in the area.

After you've prepared a worksheet, answer these questions:

1. What important changes have occurred in the neighborhood around our church building in the last five years?

2. What important changes will occur in this neighborhood in the next five years?[5]

At this point you are simply gathering data. Try not to feel overwhelmed. You are making lists of *possibilities for ministry*. Such surveys help people who have lived in a community for a while and who have grown accustomed to the landscape to see needs or changes they may not see otherwise.

One church located in a quiet suburban community was convinced that they needed to do mission in the inner city because "there were no problems where we live." A member of the social concerns committee invited a social worker to lunch to discuss a mission program downtown. Ironically, the social worker told her instead about a critical need in the church's own community. That church later sponsored a substance-abuse program for teenagers.

Invite a social worker to lunch. Go visit the local community center or social services office. What you will find are people eager for support. A local ministry in itself is caring for social workers and other people who provide care. Invite them to your church and let them tell their story.

Pastors who visit people should be encouraged to report on their visitations. This does not mean breaching confidentiality, but it does mean communicating about how people in the congregation are doing. On my rounds of the community I have been asking people about their access to health care. Simple questions asked in one community—"Do you have health insurance?" "Do you have a regular doctor?" "What do you do when your child gets sick?"—revealed a startling lack of available medical care. Pastors visit and talk with people in their homes and nursing care centers, at hospitals, corner stores, and restaurants. Ask for their impressions about what is going on around town.

Information about your community can also come out of worship. In many small churches, that part of the service devoted to "concerns of the church and community" is an opportunity to hear and ask what is happening around town. Listen carefully to what people say about factories slowing down or the need for a day-care center. Listen to peoples' prayer requests for clues about the needs of senior citizens or teenagers with nothing to do. One of our small churches developed an outreach ministry called HYMNS, Help Your Many Neighbors Service, after we learned during worship about how infrequently older villagers got to the nearest town for grocery shopping.

As you gather information about your town, begin to jot down what is missing. What needs of your community are not being met? In our early example, Grace Church discovered the need for ministries with children. Like the people at

Grace Church, think big at the outset and do not be too concerned about the "how to." What is important is that you are beginning to see your neighborhood in a new way.

In gathering information, you have described what you know about your neighborhood, and you have learned much about the culture of the community. Now you know more about how things get done, who lives around you, where people go to work. You have gained an understanding of the needs of your community. This data is a list of the *possibilities for ministry* available to your congregation. Now we focus our attention on discovering the strengths of your church, its *potential* for discovering its own unique call to community ministry.

Step 2: Understand Your Congregation's Story

After gathering information about possibilities for ministry within your community, you need to discover your congregation's *potential for ministry* in the community. Simply put, you do an inventory of your church's life. This inventory includes tangible elements like people and buildings and money, as well as intangibles like history and memory. Churches have personalities. They are gifted in very particular ways.

One of the joys of serving in a cooperative parish is that the member congregations contribute different gifts to the parish. For example, one congregation loves to sing. They are a joyous worshiping community. The gift of music and worship is shared with all the other members of the cooperative through music festivals and worship services.

A new community ministry must be appropriate for the life of your congregation. The church with the strong tradition of singing and worship will naturally move to explore new ministries that reflect this strength.

In a small rural congregation, a newly called pastor heard about the longstanding "wall" that divided the church from the community. The perception around town was that the church welcomed only the "right kind" of people. And yet, the church saw itself as the "working man's church.'' Regularly the pastor visited a mill located near the church. One day while visiting during the noon hour he noticed the workers eating lunch at their work stations. He wondered why the church could not open its meeting room to the mill workers as a lunchroom. He offered to make soup and sandwiches. A simple idea. Once a month, the mill workers attend a luncheon hosted by the deacons of the church. At the beginning the pastor made the soup and sandwiches and only a few people came. But the idea caught on and today not only do mill workers come for lunch, but the postmaster, UPS delivery men, and all the workers around town make a point to attend.

The mill luncheon program has not generated many new members for the church, but that dividing wall between church and town has come down. The church is seen as a place that cares about working people. The success of the mill luncheon ministry fit the self-understanding of the congregation. Its history was as a blue-collar congregation, and so it was natural to invite the mill workers to lunch.

Churches devote little thought to their character, what makes them special. Small churches often have poor self-images because they believe they don't measure up to the culture's norms for success. They are small and struggling. For us, one of the most enjoyable aspects of parish ministry has been discovering the church's identity and then telling the story back to the congregation. As we mentioned in the section "Understand Your Community's Needs," we do not suggest lengthy congregational analysis, but do take time to make an inventory of your church's tangibles and intangibles. Here are some suggestions for topics to explore about your congregation's life.

- **Recall the Saints**

At some point a group of people got together and built your church. Those founding fathers and mothers did not go to all that work so that their church would be fighting to survive. They had a dream. Who were these people? What did they do? What was their dream? What happened to their dream?

The farms are nearly all gone from a once-prosperous dairy farming community. The elms on Elm Street have all died. A lovely white colonial church is all that remains of a proud community. But within the congregation, now only a handful of people, there are eighty-year-old members who remember the town's heritage. Another simple project: ask the children from the elementary school to make tape-recorded interviews of the town's oldest citizens. Ask another class to take their pictures and borrow their old family photograph albums. Then have the school host a heritage weekend. Children who had always heard that their town was the "end of the line" see and hear a new story. The old ladies from church are transformed into granddaughters of farmers who long ago cleared the land.

Who comes to church now? Today's members of Old First Church who were descendants of the original settlers might see themselves as town "fathers and mothers" and might not feel comfortable with a "hands-on" mission project. But they might support a scholarship program to send a low-income person to college. A church composed of people in the trades might feel very comfortable spending a weekend on a Habitat for Humanity project. It all depends on who you have in church.

- **Recall the Tradition**

Your church has a story. Why was it founded? Who were the people who came to church and what did it mean to them? What was the community like? What are the memorable occasions in the church's history? What were its proudest moments and its low points? Has the church struggled through a crisis?

The session of a white, middle-class Presbyterian church located in an inner-city neighborhood asked us to meet with them because the church was losing members. In a decade the neighborhood had changed dramatically from ethnic German to Hispanic. The church was declining because its traditional constituency had moved to the suburbs. We asked each member of the session when they joined First Church. Most of the elders had been baptized in the church over sixty years before. Their families had immigrated to the city to work in textile mills, and the German church had been a refuge for their families. Theologically, they identified primarily with the biblical stories of the Exodus. As outsiders, we were able to suggest that their story was being repeated in the new wave of Hispanic immigration to the city. An approach to revitalizing the church would include welcoming the new immigrants; a common meeting place would be around the Exodus story and their shared experience of coming to a new land.

A church community that is working hard to keep its doors open often remembers the past as a "golden age," a time when the now sparsely occupied sanctuary was filled to capacity. They compare themselves to a mythical past and come up wanting. As you remember the saints of your congregation's past and recall the traditions that shaped your life, keep in mind that you are not seeking to repeat that past, but to discover in it clues that shape your identity today. Stories about the saints, traditions, and the way you do things are deeply embedded patterns in your congregation's life.

• **Build on the Church's Theological Tradition**

Every church has a unique tapestry of theological conviction woven of threads from its religious heritage, traditions, and people. As Carl Dudley has noted, "A theological tradition grounded in a Biblical faith is the basic identity of every congregation."[6] It is fascinating to take a well-known passage of Scripture and hear how different congregations interpret it in light of their own life.

A young pastor is called to serve a small church in a West Virginia coal mining town. As he gets acquainted with the community, he is reminded of Third World countries and the liberation theology he has studied in seminary. Surely this is the place to establish a community-based organization to begin to work for change. He preaches from Luke 4 on the liberation of the captives and freedom of the oppressed. His sermons describe worker-owned cooperatives. The congregation is polite, but no one seems interested. One Sunday at the door of the church, the oldest member asks the pastor to preach salvation and sing Wesley hymns.

The new pastor made an assumption that he did not first check out. He assumed that because the church was located in a poor, troubled place, the congregation would be sympathetic to his theological understanding of liberation theology. The congregation, however, had a very different theological understanding of itself.

Small congregations that sponsor strong community programs have a strong theological self-understanding. They are churches with a clear identity and sense of purpose. The people of the Leeds church in rural Maine can tell you their mission statement in a sentence: "To bring the gospel to the last house on the last road." They quote favorite Scripture passages from Luke concerning the Great Commission and from Ephesians about "equipping the saints" for ministry. This identity is constantly reinforced in sermons, Bible studies, and the program of the church.

The place where the stories of the saints, the traditions of the congregation, and the church's theological convictions take on life and are most apparent is in worship. A favorite hymn is the reminder of a saint who sat with her family in a particular pew and served as Sunday school superintendent for four decades. A Communion chalice brought from Scotland reminds the congregation of its immigrant heritage. A baptismal font is a reminder of the scores of children who have passed through the doors of the sanctuary. A call to renewal of baptismal vows at the end of a service says much about theological conviction.

• **Build on Today's Resources**

We have suggested some ways to identify highlights of your congregation's history. Now you need to inventory your congregation's current resources. These resources include:

People: Who in your congregation can do the work? Who are the leaders that you can call upon? Are there people in the surrounding community you can recruit to help? What skills do people have that you can call upon?

Money: Money is not everything, but it can help. What financial resources are available to your ministry? Denominational grants? Endowment funds? Community resources like the United Way?

Buildings: Many community ministries need a place to meet. Can your church make meeting space available for community groups like Alcoholics Anonymous? Could a day-care center meet in a Sunday school wing?

Gifts: What other kinds of resources are available to your congregation? In rural areas, the Cooperative Extension offers many educational programs, even consultants to help with specific projects. Colleges and universities offer resources for the community. People in your church can bring skills and insights from their work at hospitals, libraries, schools, businesses, governmental agencies, or farms. Find out what is available to your project, often at little or no cost.

Denomination: Denominational offices are often eager to lend support to new local congregational ministries, but no one ever asks for help. Find out what is available from your conference, presbytery or regional office.

In this section you have thought about the story of your congregation in all its particularity, which is part of what we call its *potential for ministry.* Now it is time to begin to think about what kind of community ministry matches your congregation's potential. Community ministry grows out of the life of the congregation. It fits the church's self-understanding. The "art" of leading your church into community ministries is finding what you are called to do in ministry.

Step 3: Define the Need Your Congregation Can Meet

The first step you have taken is to discover *possibilities for ministry* in your community. You may feel overwhelmed by the scope of the needs around you and decide you are totally ill-equipped to address them in any meaningful way. Everybody—inside the congregation and out—has been saying all along, "Our church is too small to make any impact." Sometimes embarking on a community study that highlights a range of needs can be self-defeating. "We can't do all of it so don't do any of it." But don't get discouraged. You have taken the first step and done useful work.

The second step taken was to inventory your congregation's *potential for ministry* in the community. You have completed your church's story, remembering the saints and recalling key moments in your history. You have inventoried available human and material resources. In reviewing your church's story, you might wonder what you have to contribute to the community in ministry. But keep in mind the story of LeChambon—what a poor, mountain parish of small farmers gave to several thousand Jewish refugees.

We have found it helpful for congregations to distinguish between "service ministries" and "advocacy ministries." A "service ministry" might involve organizing a community food closet or thrift shop. These types of ministries cluster around meeting people's needs. An "advocacy ministry" focuses on community justice issues. Such a ministry might be protesting living conditions for migrant workers or meeting with the school board to increase support for special education.

Now the creative work of the process begins. This is the critical step. To discover your community ministry you need to match the community's *possibilities* with the congregation's *potentials*.

We suggest listing *potentials* on one sheet and *possibilities* on another. Place them side-by-side and put together the matches. Ask yourselves, "What do we feel called to do?" Let the Holy Spirit work! Remember that you cannot take on everything you have identified on the *possibility* list. No congregation, large or small, has sufficient resources to tackle all the needs around them. But what you can do is identify one part of a community concern that fits your church's life and make it your own.

The block around Grace Church was beset by overwhelming needs. Trying to respond to all the problems facing the neighborhood would mean that nothing would be accomplished. From the entire range of needs, Grace Church selected one area to focus upon—ministry to children. Building on their long tradition of vacation Bible school, the church began an outreach to the community by inviting neighborhood children. That summer over one hundred children attended vacation Bible school. The vacation Bible school organized by Grace Church was a "service ministry." An advocacy project they might have selected could have been to meet with city officials to open schools for summer programs.

The goal of the process we have described is to discover a community ministry that your church feels called to begin. Discovering your church's ministry is a creative and dynamic process of factoring in your congregation's unique blend of history and people to meet the community's needs at a particular time and place.

Make a list of *opportunities for ministry* that look like a good match between your *potentials* and your *possibilities*. Talk about the opportunity list and try to come to a consensus about those which most closely fit your church. And ask yourself the most important question, "What do we feel called to do?"

Now you have selected a project that fits your church and you are excited about beginning. The next steps in our process involve planning to help you get started. Planning is as critical to the success of your project as the careful way in which you chose your project. We want to highlight how to take your project from the drawing board stage to actually doing it. You will need committed leadership, a clear vision of what you are doing, and adequate resources. Careful planning is important.

Step 4: Identify the Leadership to Make Your Ministry Go

Small churches actively engaged in local community ministry have strong lay and ordained leaders. A church that plans to engage in local mission will need leaders who are committed to the program and who can carry it themselves as it develops and takes root in the congregation. We suggest

recruiting a handful of people who feel called to such ministry, rather than trying to place leadership in a church board or
committee that might or might not be as committed. Pastors
and lay people need to work closely together in developing
community ministries. If pastors lack support from a few
dedicated people they will burn out in their efforts to establish the program; if lay people work without pastoral leadership they will miss the encouragement needed to keep to the
task.

• **The Role of the Pastor**

Establishing Trust: In small churches it takes several years for
the pastor to build a level of trust within the congregation before beginning to make changes. The early years of a pas-
torate must be spent in building relationships and getting to
know the community. In small churches the pastor is first a
"lover," and second a manager. Understanding the church
and community means time spent in kitchens and at lunch
counters. To be an effective small-church pastor means paying dues. Only as the congregation gets to know the minister
will they listen and be responsive to new directions.

Articulating the Vision: We believe it is fundamental for the
pastor to understand clearly the vision that helps define the
community mission of the local church. The minister needs to
be able to articulate and defend that vision through preaching, teaching, and leadership. But before pastors can lead the
congregation in social ministry, they need to have a clear
sense of themselves and their own understanding of their
pastoral role.

Participating in Mission: If pastors want their congregations
to become involved in food closets or participate in housing
rehabilitation ministries, they need to be willing to get their
hands dirty by moving food boxes or hammering nails. The
vision for local mission that you want your church to embrace
must be a top priority for pastoral leadership. Pastors serving
small churches are missioners more than they are managers.
The minister needs to take the lead in mission.

Leading the church in social ministry can prove to be a wonderful way to keep the pastor's ministry fresh and alive. The outreach programs of the churches we have studied moved congregations in directions that they could not have imagined at the outset. As a direct result, the pastor learned skills and developed expertise in subjects that were useful both to the church and to the larger community. New skills enhance a pastor's sense of calling. The pastor becomes a community asset, someone the community looks to for leadership.

Ministers can take many different leadership roles. They can be the "visionary" who comes up with ideas that are then developed and implemented by others. Or they can become expert in one area of ministry and develop several new programs in that area. What is important is that the minister of the small church participates.

Taking Risks: Becoming involved in social ministry means risking failure. The pastor's own self and reputation are on the line. Planning to begin a community ministry is critically important, but that point of decision must come when the pastor or lay leader says, "Let's do it!" and the pastor preaches the sermon laying out the new ministry to the congregation. Now the pastor is committed and must see the program through. Even with the best planning process, there are no guarantees that the program will go smoothly, and the pastor must be prepared for all eventualities.

Finding Support: Leadership in community ministry can be stressful. As churches take on community ministries they are moving into territory that is uncharted for them. Pastors often feel that in this leadership role they are climbing out onto a limb that could easily be cut. Pastors need support. The pastor who takes the lead in developing the plan for the ministry needs a safe setting to talk through the project, a place to express hopes and frustrations, and a forum to hear ideas and criticisms of others. The church planning group is not the place for this support. Better settings are gatherings with local clergy and meetings with staff of social service agencies. The

staff of our cooperative parish meets regularly to provide just
this type of support. Leading community ministries can be
lonely, and ministers need support from trusted peers.

• **The Role of the Layperson**

One of the most exciting moments in the life of a congregation is when laypersons catch hold of a vision for their church
and follow it. As pastors who have developed community
ministries, we find one of the most satisfying aspects of the
work is supporting laypersons as they develop leadership
skills and take on responsibilities they would have never
imagined for themselves.

Identifying a Critical Mass: We believe there is a critical mass
in the number of people needed to carry out a new ministry.
At the beginning of the project, the leadership might be only
a few, the minister and one or two laypersons. For example, a
crisis in the community has convinced you to respond with
concrete actions. Or through study you feel called to begin a
project in your community. The time is right. You are prepared to carry the burden personally for a period of time. You
are ready to take the risk. Good. Get to work. At some point
your group will have to think about enlisting others to help. If
you go it alone, in time you will burn out, or the project will
not be supported by the church.

Two critical masses must first be identified: that group of
workers who will support your undertaking and supportive
people in the congregation. Remember, it is not essential that
every person in the church agree with or join in what you are
proposing to do, but there needs to be a critical mass that understands the project to be the ministry of their church.

In small churches where everybody is already committed to
several responsibilities, it is sometimes hard to recruit volunteers. There are also situations where the church fully en-
dorses your new project, but no one in the congregation has
the skills to work with you in that area. Consider recruiting
people from outside the church community. The project can
still belong to your congregation, but will depend upon leaders recruited from other churches or the community at-large.

When you share a vision for how the church can respond to a need, be it a crisis or a chronic situation, it is surprising how many people will offer their help. You may think you are all alone, when in reality there are many others who share the vision and who will respond enthusiastically to the project.

A good example of the importance of having a critical mass is the story of the Leeds church housing ministry. In the start-up phase of the project, the housing ministry focused on small repair jobs. Organization was informal. The deacons would insulate a house or build a chimney. The first critical mass came when a few skilled people volunteered to work together. The second came at the point when although not everyone in the congregation felt called to hammer and saw, most approved of the project and understood the ministry to be vital to the life of the Leeds church. The program grew, and more ambitious housing projects were proposed. Congregational leaders began expressing concern about the drain on their financial and volunteer resources. Neighboring communities were requesting help with their housing problems. A new organization was needed.

In planning the new organization, church leaders wanted to continue to draw upon the support of the church, but allow other groups to join the work and expand financial resources outside of the church. They envisioned a privately incorporated, nonprofit, social service ministry encompassing several communities. The strength of this new structure was that the sponsored ministries were seen as part of the work of the Leeds church. Interested church members were encouraged to join the new organization, but no one was compelled to support the programs. In this structure the first critical mass of workers from the church was increased by broadening the base with volunteers from other communities, and the second critical mass of church support was assured by not overburdening the congregation.

Recruiting and Training Volunteers: When recruiting volunteers, be clear about what you are asking them to do. If you are organizing a day-care center in your church, recruit a vol-

unteer to do a particular job such as preparing lunch or monitoring activity on a playground. Be clear about the job and the
time commitment you are asking.

Second, provide good training for volunteers. A parents'
support group sponsored by a small town church was having
difficulty getting off the ground. Many people expressed interest in attending such a group, but no one was coming forward to act as the group leader. When professional training
was offered to anyone who would be willing to facilitate the
group, though, there were plenty of takers. Whether you are
organizing a week-long vacation Bible school or planning a
year-long day-care program, when you are relying on volunteers to work in the program always provide training and support for your staff.

Third, just as clergy who are active in social ministry need
support, so do lay leaders. A crucial role for the minister is
supporting people who are engaged in social ministries. A
simple action like attending meetings keeps communication
open and morale high. Another way to support lay leaders is
to organize informal networks of people who are working in
the same field. In Maine, coordinators from several low-
income housing ministries that are spread out over a large ge-
ographic area meet monthly for lunch to discuss their work.

Community ministries are opportunities for lay people to
discover and use their God-given talents, skills, and gifts. In
our vision for the small church, it is a place where lay and
clergy work together in what James Fenhegan has described
as "mutual ministry."

Step 5: Develop a Vision to Inspire

Community ministries grow out of a theological understanding of the mission of the church. The church of Le-
Chambon did not one day decide it would be a good idea to
be a refuge for Jews. Rather, the theological understanding of
the congregation was focused on "hospitality": God in Christ
welcomed sinners into the Kingdom, therefore the church
was called to be welcoming to strangers. When the first Jew-

ish refugees knocked on the pastor's door, they were welcomed into his home. The ministry of the LeChambonese to Jews fleeing deportation was founded on a theological understanding of the mission of the church. Their heroic actions in saving the lives of thousands of people were simply part of what it meant for this congregation to be the church. The parishioners did not view their response as anything particularly unusual.

Identifying a focus of ministry and planning well are not enough to establish a new program in the life of your congregation. If your undertaking is to touch the heart of your church, it must be grounded on the bedrock of its theological self-understanding.

In every case we have studied of small churches that are actively involved in outreach ministries, the people involved have a clear vision of why they are doing the ministry. They can quote a key scriptural passage through which they understand their ministry, or they can talk about their own experience of God's blessing in their lives. Their sustaining vision is not theoretical; it touches the heart.

Identifying and developing the vision that will inspire your community ministry is an important step in the process of planning. It can be accomplished in a number of ways.

Preaching: As you plan your ministry, don't overlook the value of sermons by the pastor or by the lay leaders to describe the new project and lift up the vision for the mission of the church.

Bible Study: Take advantage of a Bible study class to lead a series of discussions on the gospel and community ministry. Get people talking about your new ministry. Listen to their questions and concerns and use these opportunities for teaching and witness.

Lifestyle: Actions speak louder than words. Demonstrate by your lifestyle and the lifestyle of the church that community ministry is an extension of your understanding of discipleship.

Developing a vision that inspires people to action is intentional. The theological character of the congregation is deeply embedded in all aspects of the church's life. But your role in this step of the process is to state the vision and give it life in terms of your new ministry. Remember the proverb, "Without vision, the people perish."

Step 6: Build Cooperation That Leads to Lasting Results

Who will do your community ministry? Is the program going to be sponsored solely by your congregation, or are you going to seek partners for the undertaking? If a similar project is being done by another church or social agency, is there a role for you in that organization? One key to your planning is figuring out where your project fits in.

• **Church-sponsored Ministries**

Small churches that use their imagination and creativity can successfully sponsor community ministries. Over dinner at a gathering of small-church clergy, a newly ordained pastor learned about how a rural church mailed a packet of vegetable seeds with the church newsletter. She liked the idea and expanded upon it by sending out a packet of seeds to everyone in the village, as the first sign of spring. Neighbors responded enthusiastically and offered to help older residents plant the seeds in gardens. In a year a community garden program was launched, and the church reinstated an old annual service, Rural Life Sunday. A community ministry was born, a church rejuvenated.

Projects like sending out a packet of seeds cost little and pay wonderful dividends for congregations. Each year people in the village began to look forward to receiving the church newsletter containing the packet of seeds. The minister was identified as "the preacher of the church that sends out seeds to everyone."

A project for a new community ministry should not exceed your congregation's resources. Plan a project that has a defined time period with a beginning, middle, and end. Setting clear limits for projects will quiet the nerves of unsure people and not commit the congregation for an extended period of time. If the project is a success, celebrate; if it is a bust, figure out why and try again.

Where will the money come from for your new ministry? Financially, most small churches are just making it, raising money in creative ways to pay the minister and keep up the building. In the earlier steps of this process you have inventoried your financial resources. If you don't have adequate funds for the new ministry, be as creative here as you are in raising the church budget. We have found that when the need is clear for your ministry, people will support it. So ask. You might be amazed by the generosity of people you never suspected of being interested in a community project.

Ask your local newspaper or radio station to print or air a story about your project. Local news media are always on the prowl for new and interesting "human interest stories." Give people outside of your congregation the opportunity to share in your project.

• **Coalitions**

But what if your group is called to embark upon a ministry that is simply too large for the congregation's resources? In those cases we believe small churches should become partners in coalitions with other churches and social service agencies to accomplish their common mission.

Churches of all sizes have a "lone ranger" mentality. We are used to doing things on our own. We say, "If we can't do it by ourselves, we won't do it at all," or "We could never work with the Pentecostal church across town," or "We don't trust that welfare agency located in city hall." Entering into partnerships with other groups takes work, risk, and trust, but great things can happen.

In nearly every community—rural, urban, or suburban—there are social service agencies. These include federal agencies that distribute food stamps and public health services, and state and local agencies such as Aid for Dependent Children (AFDC), Women-Infant-Children (WIC), and Planned

Parenthood. As part of the fact-finding research of under-standing the needs of your community (step 1), get to know the services available in your area.

Social service agencies that serve poor people tend to be in-visible in the community, just like their clients, who are invis-ible because they are powerless. The clients are people who usually do not vote, have little economic clout and don't make waves. Spend an afternoon at your local food stamp of-fice; sit in the waiting room, read the tattered magazines, and take a look at the people who come through the door. Seldom are they the people who come through the doors of our churches.

As we suggested earlier, take a social worker to lunch. So-cial service agencies need friends. Ask what their needs are and how your church can help. Share your ideas for a better community. You will be surprised by the positive response.

Social service agencies are always looking for qualified people to serve on boards and advisory panels. A simple and very effective idea for a mission project is to volunteer at an agency. Offer to babysit children for parents completing an Aid for Dependent Children application form. Frequently, no existing agency is doing the kind of mission that you see a need for. If you have a few committed people, there are no barriers for a small church to lead in establishing a coalition of churches or social service agencies to organize a new institu-tion.

In a very small rural community, two retired school teachers saw the need for senior citizen housing. They had visited a new HUD-sponsored senior citizen housing complex in a much larger community and wondered why their community could not have one as well. They asked their local Methodist church to be the "supporting agency." The church agreed. It took a few years, but these two women built a powerful coali-tion of rural senior citizens who pressed HUD for housing. With fierce determination and patience, the group overcame incredible hurdles and setbacks. And they prevailed. Today their town is home for twenty units of senior housing.

Organizing a coalition-based social service ministry takes particular skills. You need someone good at group process, a lawyer or someone experienced in writing up bylaws and nonprofit incorporation papers, and someone to file complex IRS tax-exemption forms. But it can be done! The value of forming a coalition is the availability of more resources and ideas to expand your vision.

• **Ecumenical Councils of Churches**

Councils of churches are natural partners for developing mission projects. Our experience in working with ecumenical groups is that it is important to bring your vision to the council and let the body develop their response together. It doesn't work to bring to a council a project well along in its development and ask for support. Groups need to be able to "buy in" to a project, to make it their own. The shortcoming to this approach is that it may reduce "your congregation's sense of ownership and commitment to the ministry program."[7] Nevertheless, we believe that building coalitions and listening to diverse points of view makes for stronger and healthier undertakings in the long run.

Earlier we mentioned how a crisis in one rural town prompted the formation of a housing coalition of social service agencies and churches. For over a decade a church located on the fringe of that small town had had a ministry of visitation to a neighborhood called the "ghetto." The ghetto, or 82 High Street, was home for over fifty poor families. The saying heard around town was that you could get anything you wanted at the ghetto, from drugs to a place to sleep.

One afternoon while visiting some residents, the pastor learned that the block was up for sale and that a community group was interested in buying the street and "cleaning it up" by demolishing the trailers and apartment buildings and converting the block into a park. The family the pastor was visiting told him that they could not afford to live anywhere else in town.

With the support of our local Community Action Agency, the small church proposed that a coalition of community churches buy the block and rehabilitate it into safe, affordable, low-income housing. With a slide projector and a rough budget, the pastor began the rounds of area churches, making presentations to congregations and boards. At first churches were dismayed about the conditions of people living down the street, but they wondered what role the religious community had in redeveloping housing. After a series of meetings where we brought in representatives from communities that had done similar projects, and with the support of local and state agencies, the mood shifted from discouragement to excitement.

After a year of careful planning and nearly weekly meetings, a coalition of eight churches and several agencies bought the neighborhood and began the large task of rehabilitation. Thousands of volunteer hours were invested in the neighborhood. For the first time, churches acted "politically" by sending blocks of people to town meetings to insure passage of bills appropriating funds to the project. The religious community felt empowered by the project.

The successful redevelopment of 82 High Street was not the result of any one church's effort, but was entirely an ecumenical undertaking. Church people who otherwise would have no forum for coming together worked side-by-side on committees and on rehabilitating the buildings. Two years after we first learned about the proposed sale of 82 High Street, several hundred people packed a sanctuary to celebrate our accomplishment.

The church talks a lot about being the body of Christ. Through social ministry projects like 82 High Street, we actually had the opportunity to "become what we are."

• **Cooperative Parishes**

One of the most telling descriptions of why small churches are locked into a struggle for survival is detailed in the book *Patterns of Parish Leadership*.[8] The authors of this book carefully analyzed the cost of pastoral leadership for three mainline denominations, and found the average cost of supporting a pastor to be $30,000 per year. The implication of this finding for small churches is that most of their budgets are spent paying for their ministers. No wonder small churches operate with a "survival mentality," when most of the congregation's resources are spent paying the pastor's salary and little is left for doing ministry. Churches need to think creatively about new patterns of parish leadership.

Every village and town in the rural area where I live is marked by abandoned church buildings. Most of these parishes closed not because of lack of mission, but because they simply could not afford a full-time pastor. Rather than look for new models for leadership, the churches closed. The sparse resources of small churches will always limit their capacity to engage in community ministry—and sometimes even close their doors entirely—unless they begin to develop new ways of doing ministry.

One model for pastoral leadership that after fifty years in existence is gaining renewed interest by denominational leaders is that of the cooperative parish. A cooperative parish is created when "several congregations that share a common neighborhood or region covenant together to envision that parish area as the place in which Christ is calling them into cooperative planning and ministry."[9]

The advantages of a cooperative parish are that it makes more resources available to small congregations, and it defines "a common neighborhood or region" as the setting for ministry. The cooperative parish that I serve owns and operates a summer camp. The twelve member churches work together to sponsor a Christian camping program for low-income children in our region. None of the churches could afford to operate the camp, but all of the congregations working together provide the resources and share in the pride of accomplishment.

At a recent meeting of our cooperative parish, members of a very small rural church described the lack of adequate health care for low-income people in their area. The particular problem was that children were not being inoculated or regularly followed by a physician. The church that raised the concern had few resources other than compassion to deal with the issue. But the cooperative was able to respond by hiring a part-time parish nurse who organized "well-child clinics" in that county. The clinic was held in the small church that expressed this vital need.

In many cooperative parishes the ministers of the participating churches work together as a staff team. Congregations benefit from the skills of a team that can offer specialized services. In our cooperative parish, staff members provide resources to congregations by offering Christian education workshops, lay leadership training courses, and substance-abuse counseling. The cooperative parish also encourages staff vocational development and skills training. The staff meets together weekly for Bible study, continuing education, mutual support, and planning the work of the cooperative. Our experience suggests that when ministers serving a cooperative parish work together as a staff team, the result is more consistent and higher quality leadership.

Congregations that participate in a cooperative parish also benefit from a setting that allows people to encounter greater theological diversity in expressions of the Christian faith, while they come together in support of their common mission. An elder of a small rural church said of her cooperative, "I know every Sunday when I attend worship that there are at least twelve other churches remembering my church in their prayers. That gives me strength."

Organization for doing community ministry is critically important. Cooperative parishes provide the critical mass to do things while not sacrificing the unique qualities of small churches. As you plan your community ministry, take into account the setting most appropriate for your project. Is the project best located within the congregation, or does it need the resources of a cooperative environment?

We have given considerable attention to describing six steps to identify your community ministry and do the planning necessary to implement it. Faith is action by which you move away from that place where you are comfortable and secure to the unknown. Engaging in community ministry is always an act of faith. It is both exciting and frightening. We can suggest ways to help you think about new ministries for your church, but only you can take the step that is a leap of faith.

Getting Started with Your Community Ministry

Now is the crucial moment. Your group has done its homework. You have met regularly and studied the possibilities for service within your community. You have inventoried your church's potential for ministry. Your working group has come up with a list of possible ministries that feel right, that fit your congregation. You have put together a plan on how to go about doing your ministry. You have thought about who is going to do the work, chosen a setting, and come up with some resources. Now it's time to look around the table and have everyone say, "Let's get started!" So, let's get started.

We know of a small church that worked for over a year developing a plan to start a small business. How did they move from the planning stage to opening the doors? The critical moment happened when the organizing committee voted to spend $2,000 to buy a piece of machinery. Up to that point, the project was theoretical. When money was spent to buy a press, the project got underway. All the pieces of the puzzle of actually starting fell into place after that decision was made.

• Begin with a Guaranteed Success

If this project is your group's first experience in moving beyond church walls to do ministry, make sure your initial project is a great success. Make the first project straightforward. We suggest that first projects have clear time frames with beginnings, middles, and endings.

Remember that Grace Church, for example, planned for a community vacation Bible school of one week in length. The pastor personally visited homes in the community to invite children to the school. Teachers were carefully recruited and trained. One hundred children attended the vacation Bible school and the program was a great success.

When the Leeds church began a housing ministry, they did not start by building a new house. They spent a Saturday insulating one that was rundown. The project they chose was not controversial. Everyone in the church sympathized with the family's need. Everybody was a winner.

As you start your community ministry, work to build the confidence of people who have taken a risk. Celebrate!

• **Build on Success**

One of the strengths of doing community ministry in small churches is that you can avoid a lot of organizational structure. If your group has discovered a project that fits well within the life of the congregation, and if you have the resources, just get started.

As we have suggested, start with a manageable project that can be accomplished in a convenient time frame. When the project has been completed, evaluate it. Did it meet your expectations? What were the problems? How did the congregation and the community respond? What would you do differently?

If you have responded to a community crisis, your work may be accomplished, but your group might be just beginning its work. The success of the vacation Bible school at Grace Church led to an after-school program, and the Saturday spent repairing a poor family's house in rural Leeds, Maine, led to an organized housing ministry. What is exciting about community ministry is that you don't know where beginnings will lead you. If your ministry grows and begins to require more resources and volunteers, then you will need to think about organizational structure.

But get started. Even if not every detail is worked out, get started. In every community ministry there comes that moment when, as at the church of LeChambon, someone in need knocks on the door. Do you let them in or turn them away?

Impact on the Life of the Church

"People in the community are amazed at what the church is doing," was the appraisal of a member of a small rural church in upstate New York that had joined a cluster of churches organized around community ministries. "Overall, the people started in despair, with the church in disrepair and not enough members. They now have an enormous sense of hope—they see that they can do things. There is empowerment. Leadership is developing. The spirit is there."[10]

Social ministries can make an enormous impact for good upon the life of a small church. Churches that launch social ministries discover an identity and a sense of purpose. Members begin speaking with a sense of pride and accomplishment about the new spirit. The usual small-church problems—lack of money, few members, neglected buildings—remain, but as the church member stated, the church that sees that they "can do things" has moved beyond survival. The church has a new identity no longer fixed on the troubles, and the nagging problems take care of themselves.

The chapter "The Challenges and Opportunities Social Ministry Brings to a Small Church," contributed by Douglas A. Walrath for the book *Discerning the Call to Social Ministry*, highlights the impact social ministries have on small churches.

> When a small church engages in a substantial social ministry the church is likely to become identified by that ministry. The church will then be challenged to live up to its new identity.[11]

In our culture the church is expected to uphold the status quo, and the church is tolerated when it does not interfere with matters outside the religious sphere. When the church's actions move beyond the church walls and engage the secular culture, however, reactions to the church change. By definition, community ministry moves your church group outside sacred space into the world. Don't expect everyone to support your community ministry. In fact, be prepared for criticism and organized forces working against you, as they did in this story.

> Every neighborhood has one, that house that is an eyesore, that everyone complains about. The yard is cluttered

with broken-down cars, a mean-looking dog on a chain barks constantly. No one knows much about the people who live in the house, other than they keep to themselves. When their house caught fire and burned to the ground on a cold winter's night, everyone in the neighborhood was quietly pleased. But what the neighbors didn't notice is that members of a small church a mile away stood with the family as they watched their home and possessions burn. A church telephone hotline got busy, and a family offered to put up their homeless neighbors until they could find new quarters. Clothing and food were donated. That summer, with the church's help, a new house was built on the old foundation. By fall, the congregation gathered at the new home and celebrated with a housewarming.

The family who lost their home started attending worship services, even though they didn't look or act like the rest of congregation. They were poor and they didn't know how to read, but they came to say thank you. They kept coming, this whole family, walking down the road carrying their Bibles. They joined the church: the whole family was baptized. Their presence and participation in the church was totally unexpected. The congregation was good at giving to help the poor: they never expected to receive from them. But that is what happened.

This small church learned the truth of Douglas Walrath's belief that "social ministry offers 'victims' an opportunity to become victors. They become means of grace as they join in the ministry that was a means of grace to them."[12] The congregation realized that this family had become a gift from God that had renewed their own faith.

But the neighborhood was very critical of the church for helping the family by rebuilding their home. Church members were openly confronted for spoiling the block. Because of its community ministries, the church was labeled as "liberal." Some new people were attracted to the church because of what it did, while others looked elsewhere for a church home, feeling that the emphasis on local ministry was not appropriate. But the church believed it was faithful to its calling to serve where it did and made no excuses for its outreach.

When your congregation takes the first steps in community ministry, you don't know where those steps will lead you. Our experience and the experiences of many other churches that have risked community involvement is that the road is exciting and crowded with blessings.

Strategies for Implementation

Small churches can be leaders in organizing powerful mission programs in their community. These steps will help you get started in discovering your church's calling to community ministry (see chart on page 123).

1. Understand your community's needs.

Take a social worker to lunch.

Do a windshield survey.

Talk to people; ask what has changed in the last five years.

Inventory existing resources: agencies, coalitions.

2. Understand your congregation's story.

Compile your church's story.

Who were the saints? Why did they organize your church? What did they believe?

And don't forget today. Build on today's resources: people, buildings, money, denomination.

3. Define the need your congregation can meet.

Trust in the Holy Spirit and use your imagination.

Drawing upon community needs and your congregation's story, what ministry opportunities come to mind? Make a list of possible projects.

Identify one or two projects that you feel particularly called to do and are excited about.

4. Identify the leadership to make your ministry go.

Find those persons who feel called to this ministry and let them run with it.

Enlist volunteers with energy for the project.

Train and support them well.

5. Develop a vision to inspire.

What biblical and theological stories have nurtured your congregation? Share your vision for mission from the pulpit, in Bible study classes, and in Sunday school.

Organize a potluck supper or mission fair around your project.

6. Build cooperation that leads to lasting results.

Don't go it alone. Build coalitions with other churches, social service agencies.

Develop a cooperative style of ministry.

Start with a successful project that has a clear beginning, middle, and end.

Evaluate. Count the gains and costs.

Celebrate!

STEPS TO GETTING STARTED IN COMMUNITY MINISTRY

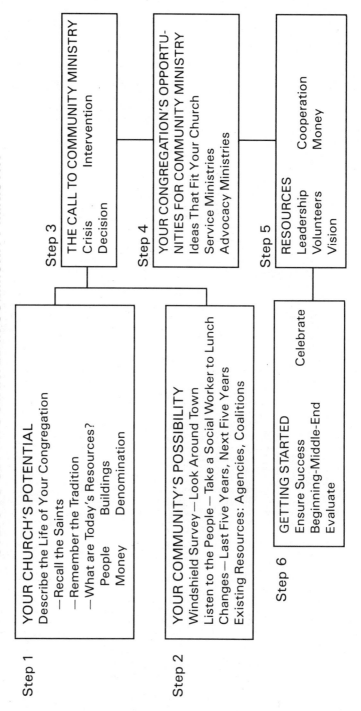

Step 1

YOUR CHURCH'S POTENTIAL
Describe the Life of Your Congregation
—Recall the Saints
—Remember the Tradition
—What are Today's Resources?
People   Buildings
Money   Denomination

Step 2

YOUR COMMUNITY'S POSSIBILITY
Windshield Survey—Look Around Town
Listen to the People—Take a Social Worker to Lunch
Changes—Last Five Years, Next Five Years
Existing Resources: Agencies, Coalitions

Step 3

THE CALL TO COMMUNITY MINISTRY
Crisis   Intervention
Decision

Step 4

YOUR CONGREGATION'S OPPORTU-
NITIES FOR COMMUNITY MINISTRY
Ideas That Fit Your Church
Service Ministries
Advocacy Ministries

Step 5

RESOURCES
Leadership   Cooperation
Volunteers   Money
Vision

Step 6

GETTING STARTED
Ensure Success   Celebrate
Beginning-Middle-End
Evaluate

Epilogue

Called to Faithfulness, Called to Action

Jesus said, "When you give a luncheon or a dinner, do not invite your friends or your . . . relatives. . . . But when you give a banquet, invite the poor, the crippled, the lame, and the blind and you will be blessed." (Luke 14:12)

My entire ministry has involved serving three small rural churches affiliated with a cooperative parish called Mission at the Eastward. Soon after I arrived in rural Maine in 1975, a tragedy struck a family living in a remote corner of the parish. James Dyer drowned on one of the last logging drives on the Kennebec River, leaving a physically handicapped wife and three small children. When I visited the widow and her children, what I saw was a poor family living in an old woods camp. At the time of his death James was rebuilding the house. The cellar was half dug. They had no money. The family needed help.

I reported the tragic story and the deplorable living conditions in this family's home at the next meeting of our cooperative parish's team of ministers. The cooperative parish director challenged me to help the family by winterizing the house. The Dyer house rehabilitation project became my first experience with community ministry.

The cooperative director had years of experience with this type of emergency need and helped me to work through each step in the project: finding out exactly what needed to be done, recruiting local volunteers, and asking for donations of materials from lumberyards. My colleague preached a sermon at my church outlining a vision for community ministry and met with the church council to talk about helping neighbors. He pledged his support and the assistance of the other parishes of the cooperative ministry.

By the end of my first summer in Maine, our small church, with the support of the cooperative parish, had winterized the Dyer's home. Our church was thrilled with its sense of accomplishment. A year later, the council proposed that we build a new house for an old man who lived in a shack. With the support of the cooperative parish, we built him a small home. The congregation was elated by their success and the good will these projects were generating in the village community.

I was hooked by community ministry. When I came to Maine I had no idea that this form of ministry would be at the center of my work. After completing a few more housing rehabilitation projects, the confidence level of the parish rose, and new areas of ministry were begun. The parish organized community thrift shops and food banks. Because of the scope of needs in our rural communities, the churches could not tackle problems alone. New projects in economic development and affordable housing were explored with the cooperative parish and with regional social service agencies.

Looking back over the years of ministry in Maine, I know I have been blessed by the opportunity to share in a cooperative parish and to learn from its director. Without their support and guidance, I am sure that I would have stayed in the parish a few years, grown restless, and moved on. But I have never felt "second class" serving small churches. To the contrary, I am confident that the innovative programs sponsored by the cooperative parish and its member churches have contributed to the life of the whole church.

Today, hundreds of volunteers from churches across the country come to Maine to work in our housing construction and rehabilitation programs. The experiences gained by these volunteers working side-by-side with low-income people renews their faith in the mission of the church. We also work with several seminaries preparing students for careers in small churches. Our message to seminarians is that ministry in small churches takes the best one has to give. We are exploring pastoral options by employing "tent-makers" and training lay leaders to serve our congregations. Working in cooperation with public health agencies, we are planning to hire a parish nurse to teach preventive health care. I feel called and very proud to serve in this cooperative parish.

Our parishes have all the problems that small churches face—lack of resources, buildings in need of repair, not enough people to do all the work—but we have never felt like we were merely surviving. We believe we are ministering to the needs of our community. Mission at the Eastward has been sustained for nearly forty years by its founding vision, "to reach the last house on the last road." The leadership of the Mission—both clergy and lay—has always encouraged the staff and the people of the churches to share an expansive vision of mission, to dream and to work hard and creatively to make those dreams practical realities. Everything that the cooperative parish has accomplished, from supporting churches in villages that could not support full-time ministries to organizing comprehensive social service programs, has been truly a cooperative effort.

At the heart of our cooperative ministry is Sunday morning worship (and serving a multichurch parish Sunday afternoon, too!). It is through worship, whether with a handful or a full house, that I keep in touch with people's needs and my own needs for spiritual renewal. Building worshiping communities is the most important part of our ministry. I am supported in my day-by-day ministry, often encountering tragic situations, by the spiritual strength of the congregations.

The community ministries sponsored by our churches and the cooperative parish have brought me and the congregations into relationships with people we would not have known but for our outreach. The Dyer family, whose home we repaired years ago, joined the small church that responded to their need. I baptized their children, watched them grow up, and officiated at their weddings. Over and over, the people we helped have helped us. Our neighbors have helped our small churches discover their mission. Reaching out to the community with ministry is risky, but the returns are great.

I encourage your congregation to take the risk and plunge into local mission. In these chapters we have described mission at four levels: Presence, People, Pattern, and Program. Each level of local mission is important. The presence of a church in a community "anchoring" the faith of a shut-in who cannot attend worship services is as much mission as highly visible outreach programs. Faithfulness in mission is more important than size. Our hope is that your congregation discovers the mission to which it is called.

This book is devoted to helping small churches understand, develop, and nurture local mission. We have argued that the newly emerging mission field is in our backyards. But what about national and international missions? Does the emphasis on local mission eliminate historic and cherished commitments to traditional mission fields? By arguing for local mission work aren't we furthering the societal drift to look inward rather than outward? These are important questions that deserve our attention.

For nearly two decades I have served in a national missions field. Our cooperative parish receives generous support from across our denomination. Women's groups send us beautifully handcrafted layettes for newborns. Churches organize benefits to purchase power tools for our housing rehabilitation program. Every day I receive letters from people who remember our parishes in their prayers. Such support is deeply moving, and continually reminds me that our ministry is a "partnership in the gospel" across the country. The nature of the support we receive is personal. The people of our churches want to be involved; they want to know that what they do matters. They want to be connected.

I believe that by participating in local mission our congregations develop a deeper appreciation for the whole mission enterprise of the church. I do not believe that local mission detracts from global mission, but rather enhances it. Local mission provides that critical sense of connection, of making a difference in another's life. My experience shows that when churches are active in local mission, they are active in mission at every level of the church.

—Scott Planting

Endnotes

Chapter 1

1. Carl Dudley, "The Character of Leadership," *The Five Stones* (Winter 1989), p. 2, adapted.

2. Differences in the perspectives of social organizations is explored more fully in Anthony Pappas, *Money, Motivation, and Mission in the Small Church* (Valley Forge: Judson Press, 1989).

3. See, for example, "A Child Shall Lead Them," *Newsweek* (December 17, 1990). On sizism, see David Ray, *Small Churches Are the Right Size* (New York: The Pilgrim Press, 1982).

4. Quoted from the film *Weapons of the Spirit.*

Chapter 2

1. Loren Mead, *The Once and Future Church*, (Washington, D.C.: The Alban Institute, 1992).

2. Emily Chandler, unpublished remarks from the National Presbyterian Small Church Celebration, August 6-9, 1992, San Antonio, Tex.

3. Mead, *Once and Future*, p. 69.

4. Anthony Pappas, *Money, Motivation, and Mission in the Small Church* (Valley Forge: Judson Press, 1989), p. 100.

5. Taylor Branch, *Parting the Waters: America in the King Years, 1954-63* (New York: Simon and Schuster, 1988), pp. 11-12.

6. Conrad Richter, *A Simple, Honorable Man* (New York: Alfred A. Knopf, 1962) pp. 101-108.

7. Parker Palmer, *The Company of Strangers* (New York: Crossroads, 1981), p. 21.

8. Ibid., p. 20.

9. Ibid., p. 136.

10. Ibid., p. 136.

11. Ibid., p. 137.

12. Ibid., p. 28.

13. Carol Bly, *Letters from the Country* (New York: Harper and Row, 1991), pp. 35-36,39.

14. John E. Biersdorf, *How Prayer Shapes Ministry* (Washington, D.C.: The Alban Institute, 1992).

15. Carl S. Dudley, "Giving Voice to Local Churches: New Congregational Studies," *Christian Century*, Vol. 109, No. 24 (August 12-19, 1992).

Chapter 3

1. This statement was apparently made by one of my ancestors, Pappus of Alexandria, in *Collectio*, Book VIII, Prop. 10, Sec. 11.

2. Jini Moore, "Churches that Model the Beloved Community," *The American Baptist* (January/February 1991).

3. John Dorean, "Growing Lives and Churches Through Hands-On Mission," *The Five Stones*, vol. 10, no. 4 (Fall 1992).

4. A more complete discussion of this aspect of small-church mission is found in *Entering the World of the Small Church: A Guide for Leaders* and *Money, Motivation, and Mission in the Small Church*, both by Anthony G. Pappas.

5. Reprinted with permission from "How Do Small Towns Work?: A Guide for New Pastors," by Richard Griffin, *Action Information*, Jan.-Feb. 1991, published by The Alban Institute, Inc., 4125 Nebraska Avenue, NW, Washington, DC 20016. All rights reserved.

6. Joseph Sastic, "Ecological Stewardship" in *Our Only Home: Plant Earth* (Valley Forge: American Baptist Churches USA, 1991), pp. 24ff.

7. See James E. Cushman, *Beyond Survival* (Parsons, W.Va.: McClain Printing Co., 1981).

8. From *The Salonnet Times*, Portsmouth, Rhode Island. Used by permission.

9. Percy Walley, Burnside Baptist Church, Burnside, Iowa.

Chapter 4

1. "A Child Shall Lead Them," *Newsweek* (December 17, 1990), pp. 52-53.

2. Paul Tsongas, *The Road from Here* (New York: Alfred A. Knopf, 1981).

3. Carl Dudley, *Making the Small Church Effective* (Nashville: Abingdon Press, 1978), cover.

4. Reprinted from *Spires* (American Baptist Churches of Maine, March 1991).

5. Contributed by Dirk Lewis Ficca, First Presbyterian Church, Benton Harbor, Michigan.

6. Report of a sermon by Christina Del Piero, pastor of St. Paul's United Church of Christ, a small, inner-city congregation in the East Bronx. Used by permission.

7. From *Prairie Fire*, report for 1991, compiled in Des Moines, Iowa.

8. Marshall Schirer, "How to Help Small Churches in Their Ministry," *The Five Stones*, vol. 1, no. 2, p. 2.

Chapter 5

1. Carl S. Dudley, *Basic Steps Toward Community Ministry* (Washington, D.C.: The Alban Institute, 1992), p. 47.

2. For information about Mission at the Eastward, write MATE, RFD #3, Box 3897, Farmington, Maine 04938.

3. For information about Grace Presbyterian Church, write Grace Presbyterian Church, 811 Benton Blvd., Kansas City, MO 64124.

4. Philip Hallie, *Lest Innocent Blood be Shed* (New York: Harper and Row, 1979).

5. Douglas A. Walrath, *Planning For Your Church* (Philadelphia: Westminster Press, 1984), p. 82.

6. Dudley, *Basic Steps*, p. 47.

7. Ibid., p. 86.

8. Dean Hoge, et al., *Patterns of Parish Leadership* (Kansas City, Mo.: Sheed and Ward, 1988).

9. *Evangelism and Church Development Handbook* (Presbyterian Church, U.S.A., 1991).

10. *Nor'easter* (January/February 1992).

11. Malcolm C. Burson, et al., *Discerning the Call to Social Ministry* (Washington, D.C.: The Alban Institute, 1990), pp. 76-77.

12. Ibid., p. 79.

Additional Resources

Action Information, The Alban Institute, 4125 Nebraska Avenue, NW, Washington, D.C. 20077-4904.

Biersdorf, John E., *How Prayer Shapes Ministry* (Washington, D.C.: The Alban Institute, 1992).

Bly, Carol, *Letters from the Country* (New York: Harper and Row, 1981).

Branch, Taylor, *Parting the Waters: America in the King Years 1954-63* (New York: Simon and Schuster, 1988).

Briggs, William, *Faith Through Works* (Franconia, N.H.: Thorn Press, 1983).

Burson, Malcolm C., et al., *Discern the Call to Social Ministry* (Washington, D.C.: The Alban Institute, 1990).

Burt, Steve, *Activating Leadership in the Small Church* (Valley Forge, Pa.: Judson Press, 1988).

Carroll, Jackson W., ed., *Small Churches Are Beautiful* (San Francisco: Harper and Row, 1977).

Cushman, James E., *Beyond Survival* (Parsons, W.Va.: McClain Printing Co., 1981).

Dudley, Carl S., *Basic Steps Toward Community Ministry* (Washington, D.C.: The Alban Institute, 1991).

Dudley, Carl S., ed., et al., *Carriers of Faith* (Louisville: Westminster/John Knox Press, 1991).

Dudley, Carl S. and Douglas Alan Walrath, *Developing Your Small Church's Potential* (Valley Forge, Pa.: Judson Press, 1988).

Dudley, Carl S., "Giving Voice to Local Churches: New Congregational Studies," *Christian Century*, vol. 109, no. 24 (August 12-19, 1992).

Dudley, Carl S., *Making the Small Church Effective* (Nashville: Abingdon Press, 1978).

Evangelism and Church Development Handbook (Presbyterian Church, U.S.A., 1991).

Fenhegan, James, *Mutual Ministry* (New York: Harper and Row, 1977).

Grierson, Denham, *Transforming a People of God* (Joint Board of Christian Education of Australia and New Zealand, 1984).

Griggs, Donald I. and Judy McKay Walther, *Christian Education in the Small Church* (Valley Forge, Pa.: Judson Press, 1988).

Hallie, Philip, *Lest Innocent Blood Be Shed* (New York: Harper Torchbooks, 1985).

Hoge, Dean, et al., *Patterns of Parish Leadership* (Kansas City, Mo.: Sheed and Ward, 1988).

Hopewell, James F., *Congregation: Stories and Structures* (Philadelphia: Fortress Press, 1987).

Jackson, W. Carroll, Carl S. Dudley, and William McKinnery, *Handbook for Congregational Studies* (Nashville: Abingdon, 1986).

Koenig, John, *New Testament Hospitality* (Philadelphia: Fortress Press, 1985).

Mead, Loren, *The Once and Future Church* (Washington, D.C.: The Alban Institute, 1991).

New Times, New Calls, produced by the Evangelism and Church Development Unit in cooperation with the Synod of the Sun (Presbyterian Church, U.S.A., 1991).

Palmer, Parker, *The Company of Strangers* (New York: Crossroads, 1981).

Pappas, Anthony G., ed., *The Five Stones—Newsletter for Small Churches*, P.O. Box D-2, Block Island, RI 02807.

Pappas, Anthony G., *Entering the World of the Small Church:*

A Guide for Leaders (Washington, D.C.: The Alban Institute, 1988).

Pappas, Anthony G., *Money, Motivation and Mission in the Small Church* (Valley Forge, Pa.: Judson Press, 1989).

Ray, David, *Small Churches Are the Right Size* (New York: The Pilgrim Press, 1982).

Richter, Conrad, *A Simple, Honorable Man* (New York: Alfred A. Knopf, 1962).

Tsongas, Paul, *The Road from Here* (New York: Alfred A. Knopf, 1981).

Walrath, Douglas A., *New Possibilities for Small Churches* (New York: The Pilgrim Press, 1983).

Walrath, Douglas A., *Planning for Your Church* (Philadelphia: Westminster Press, 1984).

Whyte, William H., Jr., *The Organization Man* (New York: Simon and Schuster, 1956).